# *Bereavement*

## A GUIDE TO COPING

CHRISTOPHER GOLDING

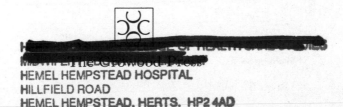

The Crowood Press

First published in 1991 by
The Crowood Press Ltd
Ramsbury, Marlborough
Wiltshire SN8 2HR

British Library Cataloguing in Publication Data

Golding, Christopher
  Bereavement : a guide to coping.
  1. Bereavement
  I. Title
  306.88

  ISBN 1 85223 438 5

**In memory of my dear mother and father,
Hazel Marion and Lloyd Douglas Golding.**

Typeset by Action Typesetting Limited, Gloucester.
Printed in Great Britain by Redwood
Melksham, Wilts.

# Contents

# Preface

My reasons for writing this book stemmed from the proximity of dying loved ones and a realization, some nine years later, that this would be a challenging subject about which to write, knowing that it can all too easily be simply brushed aside – I, at one time, being guilty of taking this very stance. Indeed, my book is hardly likely to significantly alter deeply entrenched attitudes and it may not reach the height of popular reading. However, it deals with a subject which deserves to be regarded as a topic worthy of serious study, after all, none of us can avoid it.

I have written in a way which I feel would have been of value to me during my own period of bereavement, when many questions and dilemmas faced me and to which I could find no answer. At the time there was a dearth of literature on the subject and both myself and others with whom I came into contact at the time were unaware of any such publications that existed. It is my hope, therefore, that this book will begin to assist others in finding answers to their questions.

This book is written by a layperson, thereby providing a layperson's view of bereavement. I have not written it as a professional or lay counsellor; I represent no organization and so, to this extent, I hope I have been able to provide a degree of objectivity, given the nature of the subject.

It is primarily intended for those who have undergone or are about to undergo bereavement, those who are caring for the terminally ill, those who are or will be caring for a bereaved person and those who feel that they wish to take a deeper interest in the subject, in general. The issues of disablement and the additional effects that bereavement will have in such circumstances are also considered. Further reading and details of useful organizations are provided at the end.

I do not regard my work as definitive and it is quite possible that the reader may disagree with some of the things that I have written. However, this can only be a good thing as the book is intended to provoke personal thought on the subject.

The case studies are intended to reflect realistically the multiplicity of reactions to bereavement. Some of the studies are composites, having been taken from more than one source; others are complete in themselves. However, all of them are taken from real-life situations.

The chapter headings are self-explanatory. However, it is important to mention that Chapters 7 and 8 may be especially helpful to those having to face bereavement because of an infant or child death. This is often an area of complete misjudgement and misunderstanding by others. It is hoped that a clearer view can be offered to those providing support and to clear away some of the myths that may be forced upon parents.

Penultimately, I wish to emphasize that each chapter is not to be read or to be seen in isolation. It can be the case, for example, that the points I have discussed in instances of sudden loss, may well be relevant to someone having just lost their grandparent, following a long illness.

Finally, I wish to extend my very special thanks to Rita Fraser of the Portsmouth Baby Lost Support Group, for her fine contribution in Chapter 8. Also, my special thanks to Doris Crowe, who generously provided the basis for 'A Diary to Share'.

My thanks also to Michael Marten, RN, (diver at the scene of the Zeebrugge ferry disaster), and thanks, too, to those people who agreed to be interviewed and who wish to remain anonymous.

*Christopher Golding, 1991*

# 1 What is Bereavement?

## ATTITUDES

Ask any person about his or her understanding of the word bereavement, and you may well be left in no doubt that the subject should be avoided.

Unless they have been personally touched by bereavement, very few people seem willing to discuss openly such a momentous and unavoidable part of the human experience. Many negative attitudes seem to prevail. Often, bereavement is considered something to be faced only when absolutely necessary, so until then it can safely be ignored; or perhaps it is seen as tempting fate to talk about it; maybe it is thought to be simply too morbid a subject to be contemplated. There can be little wonder that such prejudices exist when so little education on the subject is given, especially during the formative and most impressionable years of life. There is no constructive consideration of bereavement; it is left, like many other important issues, to be dealt with as and when circumstances arise. It is not being suggested, of course, that the subject of bereavement can be 'learned' in advance, but an awareness of what is involved must surely be desirable.

Childhood is the ideal starting point; children have a natural inclination to incorporate their concept of death as a part of the playing process. How often have you heard the expression 'Bang, bang, you're dead'? Again, when children lose a much-loved pet, the question of whether the animal will 'go to heaven' is usually uppermost in their minds. However, instead of taking advantage of such opportunities to pursue the question meaningfully, and (allowing for the age of the child) to explain that death is an inevitable part of life, adults

1

often fudge the issue with such put-offs as 'You will understand one day when you are older', their embarrassment plainly evident.

In *Children's Conceptions of Death,* Richard Lonetto shows that children are helped to manage their anxieties about death by drawing and by talking about the subject. Robert E. Kavanaugh in *Facing Death* stresses that the most worthwhile method of teaching children about death is to allow them to talk freely and without the usual adult rhetoric. How the discussion proceeds is not important; what is important is the learning process, and for a parent to find out the child's perception of death.

However, it is more usual that by the time most children reach adulthood the question of death and bereavement is at the bottom of the agenda. Career development and family commitments take precedence. The pressures and responsibilities of everyday life leave little time or inclination for thoughts about something that few will have yet experienced.

Perhaps another reason for our lack of interest is that, as a society, we are protected from the processes of dying, death and bereavement. They have become largely institutionalized. Often it is left to the professionals to care for those needing comfort and succour in the time of greatest need, and so the opportunity to share and witness such intimate aspects of life is either non-existent or very limited. This is in direct contrast to the beginning of the century, when the extended family unit – three generations living in the same household being by no means uncommon – experienced together the beginnings and the endings of life. It is ironic, therefore, that in this latter part of the twentieth century, society is probably exposed to more instances of death, dying and bereavement than at any other period. The media, television especially, make us witness to countless tragedies at home and abroad, and to the emotions of those caught up in such events. However, it is probably true to say that such continual exposure tends only to dull our reactions and numb our sense of shock, and that a minor incident affecting someone close to us will upset us more deeply.

2

The attitude to death and bereavement in television soap operas is an interesting reflection of society's stance. Bereavement has to be tidied up fairly swiftly so that life can resume normality; grief is liable to be seen as a bit of a nuisance, even embarrassing, perhaps, if prolonged and unconventional. Lest the ratings be affected, therefore, the characters either get over their loss as quickly as possible and return to normal, or temporarily disappear from proceedings for a decent interval. The plot makes only a token gesture to bereavement, with no attempt at understanding or portraying the reality of grief.

## A Case History: Edward

Edward, is twenty-eight and married with three children. He considers his mother and father to have been loving but over-protective parents. He recalls how the issue of bereavement, like the facts of life, had been a taboo subject as he grew up. It was regarded – if, that is, it was regarded at all – as an unpleasantness to be tackled only when force of circumstance made it necessary.

He was an only son and an only grandson, and extremely close to his grandmother, who had been widowed at an early age. She seemed to Edward to have been almost the sister he had never had, as well as almost a second mother. She had never enjoyed a robust constitution but she never complained too loudly, and as far as Edward was concerned she seemed to be the picture of health, that is up until the last few weeks of her life.

Edward was six when his mother took him to one side one day and said, 'You know that Grandma has been feeling rather poorly lately, Edward. Well, she's now had to go to her new home in the sky. But don't worry, Grandma will be thinking of you and she'll be very happy there.' At such a young age Edward had never imagined Grandma not always being near to him. His mother's words were, therefore, profoundly alarming. He was full of questions: How could Grandma have gone to a new home in the sky without telling him? Where was this new home? Didn't she like the one she had here? How did she get there? She couldn't have flown because she always said she would never go in an aeroplane. So how, why and where had she gone? He didn't know which question to ask his mother first. He felt deserted. Had he done something terrible and this was the punishment?

3

No amount of questioning elicited a satisfactory answer from his mother. He couldn't understand why the curtains at the front of the house had to be drawn. 'It's a mark of respect to Grandma,' said his mother. But if Grandma had gone away somewhere 'up there', why draw the curtains? To make matters more perplexing, people were now beginning to wear funny-looking clothes all in black. His upset and bewilderment deepened when he had to make a strange journey to what seemed like a field full of vertical stone books with lots of words on the grey covers. He wasn't allowed to see the purpose of the visit, but was told everyone had come to say goodbye to Grandma.

Edward has never forgotten his experience and is not letting his children suffer from a similar lack of explanation.

## DEFINING BEREAVEMENT

So far, no definition of the word 'bereavement' has been given. It might be felt that such a definition is unnecessary, the meaning being somewhat self-evident. But is it really? Most people would probably define it as 'a loss, by death, of a wife, husband, child, mother or similarly close relative', and that is indeed a start. However, imagine an intergalactic visitor, unfamiliar with human emotions, asking the question and receiving the same answer; it would clearly fall short of embracing the immense upheaval – emotional, mental and sometimes even physical – that can be bound up with bereavement.

The Oxford English Dictionary defines 'bereave' as 'to deprive, rob, dispossess – a powerful definition that begins to shape a more accurate picture. It conveys by implication that there will be a profound impact upon people's lives. In addition, no *exclusive* implication is made of a loss, by death, of a loved one. Thus, although bereavement will most often be considered to have this more usual meaning, it cannot be considered in isolation. In a wider context, anyone suffering from an amputation or a permanent physical incapacity may be reasonably supposed to feel deprivation, dispossession and probably a deep sense of having been robbed. To take the definition a stage further, bereavement can also include such personal crises as divorce, assault and rape.

The fundamentals of bereavement, then, embrace more than may at first be apparent, and the following chapters, although primarily concerned with bereavement as a result of a physical demise, may perhaps be read with a wider context in mind.

# 2 Reactions to Bereavement

## GRIEF IS NORMAL

Grief is a normal part of bereavement. Those who think the situation can be controlled and overcome by pulling oneself together are deceiving themselves; indeed, those who claim to be capable of doing so are probably in urgent need of assistance. Grief at some stage after bereavement is inevitable, and in clinical terms is an essential ingredient for a healthy emotional and physical adjustment.

Contemplating the potential which can never be fulfilled after the loss of a loved one is one of the most heart-rending aspects of bereavement. Age can be irrelevant. People in their seventies and eighties can be almost as active as those in middle age, so potential is not necessarily related to age. Being denied the company of the person who for so long has shared one's life seems so profoundly unjust. In the face of such a void, the heartache and pain now felt so agonizingly will, at first, seem to be there for an eternity. Life has changed irrevocably. The ship that was steering its course has now foundered, and refloating it seems an impossibility.

Being stricken with grief is not like suffering from an illness. Some can carry on their everyday lives as normal; indeed, normal activities can take on a new meaning and become a way of absorbing hitherto unrealized energy. Some may wish to engross themselves in work and hobbies; others may need to talk endlessly about the life they shared with a lost loved one. However a person's emotional make-up leads them to react, it is not for those around them to pass judgement on whether a reaction is normal or not. Those who bear the task of offering comfort can easily – and unintentionally – be led

6

into thinking that their bereaved charge is unusual or odd. This simply is not the case. Such an attitude could only be justified if grief continued unabated for many years.

Perhaps worse is the implication that the bereaved is acting selfishly: 'I went through the same trauma, but I had to come to terms with it.' If such a person did come to terms with their loss more quickly – and time can be a great distorter of accuracy – then he or she is indeed fortunate. But different people experience bereavement in different ways and there is no neat formula for getting over it. It is for others to make allowances, not for the bereaved to be anxious about the effect they are having upon those around them.

The closing of a chapter in a close relationship can be an extremely enriching experience, in retrospect. There will come a moment, after our grief has run its course, when we will realize the fullness of our experience and understand that it is because we have loved and lost so much that we have felt such heartache. We will realize that our pain has not been pointless, indeed, it will be viewed as having been irreplaceable. If it had never happened, then we really would have cause to worry.

## A Case History: Robert

Robert, 26, had been expecting the death of his father, his only remaining parent, for nearly six months, and had been intermittently distraught over that period.

When the tragic day arrived he demonstrated complete control and perfect calm. He had accepted that his father's death was inevitable, and when the moment arrived there was a feeling almost of relief at the termination of suffering, and the end seemed the most perfectly natural thing to have happened. The subsequent arrangements were carried out with military precision. Relatives offered help but found themselves virtually surplus to requirements as their nephew was in total charge. The winding up of the estate immediately after the funeral was undertaken with businesslike efficiency. The idea of instructing a solicitor seemed quite unnecessary. Robert was regarded as coping well, and the enthusiasm with which he undertook the legal side of matters was seen as good therapy by those around him. But after four weeks his composure suddenly gave way, and it became impossible for him to continue. His dear dad's existence, together with all his memories of his parent, seemed to be reduced to mere pieces of paper – bank statements and reference numbers. Professional legal help was sought and everything handed over. Robert's grief, temporarily delayed, had begun.

## OVERWHELMED IN A SEA OF ATTENTION

For all too many people, 'paying their last respects' can mean just that – and it is the last the bereaved may see of them for some time. For someone suffering the loss of a loved one, however, the funeral is usually just the beginning. Up till then so much time has been devoted to abnormal administrative tasks that the seeming unrealness of the situation can mask actuality. There are endless forms to be filled out, appointments and arrangements to be made. Receiving friends and relatives who may not have been seen for years can be very demanding, although within some families contact is so infrequent that the meeting of the clan can be positively therapeutic for a short time. The purpose of the reunion may be temporarily forgotten and one could be forgiven for thinking that it was a happy party rather than the traditional gathering following the funeral. After the hectic schedule of the days following a bereavement, culminating in the funeral itself, there may be feelings of emptiness and complete isolation. Being kept busy, with little time to reflect, may have given rise to the feeling that coping is going to be possible after all. But the rallying round of friends, neighbours and relations, and the attention paid to the bereaved, reaching a climax at the funeral, may drop away all too suddenly. Now the pieces have to be picked up, and support and understanding from those closest to the bereaved are vital.

## BODILY RESPONSES

This is a time when our bodies will be feeling at their weakest, and there may be reduced resistance to illnesses which ordinarily would pose no problem. Aches and pains may appear, together with a variety of minor symptoms having no apparent physical cause. It is a good idea to have a medical check-up even if no symptoms are apparent. A good general practitioner can offer advice and guidance during this period.

There may be a loss of weight. Normal eating patterns are likely to be interrupted, and in any case one's appetite will probably be diminished. Weight loss may be apparent even if one's usual diet is adhered to, surplus calories being used up by stress and the energy expended in coping with an unusual situation. Even though food may seem unimportant at this time, it is vital, and it should be nutritious. Those who are unused to catering for themselves, however, are likely to 'make do' with convenience foods, perhaps of a poor nutritional value, thereby contributing to the body's reduced resistance levels. It might be a good idea to seek the help of a dietician; even those who consider themselves to be eating normally may be in need of a supplement.

Sleep disturbance may well present a problem, especially during the early days of bereavement. Apart from medication, which should be treated with circumspection, there is no real formula for remedying the difficulty. Often, the sheer pressure of a sudden and drastically changed lifestyle will be exhausting in itself, leading to at least some welcome sleep. Talking with understanding friends till late at night may help the situation. Additionally, putting feelings down on paper can be a way of lightening the burden. Such writings can also be very comforting and may even give help to another person later on. Staying with a close friend or friends, or having them stay with you during the early days, is very desirable. Being able to unburden intense feelings whenever you need to will bring peace, little by little.

There may be a strong temptation to take alcohol, and in moderation this can be a comfort. The danger – and this cannot be stated too strongly - lies in using alcohol as a crutch, or as a means of trying to deaden the heartache and the pain. At first, it may seem a wonderful solution. The burden may appear to ease as the world becomes hazier, but all one is doing is delaying the inevitable as well as creating new problems. It is better to face up to reality than to seek to postpone it, with the additional risk of alcohol dependence. Women should not exceed fourteen units of alcohol a week. The limit for men is twenty-one units a week. A 'unit' is a glass of wine, or a single measure of spirits, or a half pint of average-strength beer or lager, or a small glass of fortified wine (sherry, vermouth, etc). Kept within these limits, and spread over a week – it's no good taking your limit all at once! – alcohol will be a pleasure, not a disaster. One final point: never combine alcohol with any prescribed medication. It is easy to forget with so much occupying one's mind, so if necessary, write a reminder and place it in a prominent position.

The same precepts apply to smoking. Even a non-smoker may be tempted to seek comfort from this most pernicious of habits and habitual smokers may increase their consumption, albeit persuading themselves that this is only temporary. However, trying to revert to one's previous rate of consumption, let alone attempting to give up the habit altogether, is going to be very difficult. Be strong and look at the various aids to cutting down and giving up which have appeared on the market. Better still, have a word with your GP and investigate anti-smoking group therapy meetings.

## THE EXPECTATIONS OF OTHERS

When one has experienced the death of a person with whom there has been the deepest understanding, camaraderie and love, and where that relationship has been so integral a part of one's life, attempting to convey one's feelings to others seems impossible.

Such a relationship may never have needed to be verbalized: actions and reactions may always have been enough, the smallest look, touch or gesture conveying more than a thousand words ever could. What has transpired within that relationship has been entirely private and absolutely unique to the persons concerned; what others have gleaned from it can only be, at best, a second-hand notion.

When someone close loses or is about to lose a loved one, one may feel concern not only about the bereaved person's reaction following his or her loss, but also about one's own ability to cope with a situation which may be unfamiliar, especially when called upon to fill a supportive role.

For the bereaved person, the feeling that others might have expectations about his or her behaviour can be an additional worry. The supportive caregiver will accept a bereaved person's reaction without criticism or, at least, will be careful not to let any criticism show. It is probably salutary in such a situation to imagine the roles reversed – how would one feel if, in addition to experiencing a deep loss, one had to bear the unfavourable judgements of others? The bereaved must be allowed to heal at their own pace, in their own way and over a period of time sufficient for their needs. Each person is different, and anyone genuinely offering support will realize this and adjust their response accordingly.

Some people, especially those who have not experienced the loss of someone close, seem to have particular expectations of those who have. They tend to make *ad hoc* classifications, placing the bereaved in 'minor' or 'major' categories of bereavement, and expecting from them certain predetermined modes of behaviour. Any deviation from this assumed norm may lead to puzzlement, a lessening of sympathy, and the view that the bereaved person is not behaving in the right way. It is not unusual for such people to look upon bereavement almost as an illness.

## 'A Minor Bereavement'

To those who make such classifications, this might be considered to include the loss of the very elderly, who are perhaps not immediately related – in other words, people who are assumed to have lived out their allotted span and to have had the opportunity to fulfil their ambitions. They may well consider, too, that miscarriage is a 'minor bereavement'; since the foetus never fully developed, they assume that the opportunity for a 'proper' relationship never arose, consequently only limited outward expression of loss may be expected here.

## A Case History

A young man of twenty-four who had been extremely close to his great aunt was profoundly affected by her death at the age of ninety-two. He telephoned his place of work to explain that he was unable to attend the office that day because of his grief. The following day he felt able to resume work, but upon his arrival he was promptly ordered to see his immediate superior, who reprimanded him for taking the day off. No sympathy was offered for his loss; obviously it was felt that the aunt was too distant and too elderly a relative for 'normal' emotions to apply. The circumstances certainly did not justify sick leave, and he would have to forfeit a day's pay, although he would be allowed a couple of hours off for the funeral. The important issue, as his boss saw it, was whether or not this sort of conduct was likely to be repeated, with other staff taking days off – and expecting to be paid – whenever some distant elderly relation died. No attempt was made to examine the particular circumstances, and the young man was made to feel a fraud.

However, such an inflexible attitude is patently unjust and insensitive. Why shouldn't someone feel a deep sense of loss in such circumstances? The relationship, not the proximity of blood or marital ties, is the determining factor.

## 'A Major Bereavement'

This is often seen as the loss of a close relative, especially someone who has died comparatively young, and thus been denied their 'full potential'. This category will be seen as including a parent with young children, the middle-aged, adolescents and children.

Upsetting, unhelpful, hurtful responses are utterly unintentional, but nevertheless they are often proffered. Sympathizers may feel embarrassed, awkward, or simply may not wish to risk saying the wrong thing. Consequently, their self-consciousness at being confronted by a bereaved person can lead to feelings

12

of defensiveness; some can feel threatened by a situation they would rather avoid, but they feel it is better to say anything rather than nothing at all. The situation is turned on its head, with the bereaved having to put at ease and help those who are struggling to express sympathy! Having lost a loved one, the bereaved now has the added burden of dealing with tactless sympathizers.

When one is experiencing a 'major' bereavement, others may have odd preconceptions about the bereaved's expression of grief. For example, they may presume that the bereaved person should appear continually grief stricken until a suitable time has elapsed. They may assume that unless there are frequent bouts of tears and abject depression, then the bereaved is cold and uncaring – never mind the effort involved in putting on a brave face. It also does not occur to such people that when someone expects bereavement as the inevitable outcome of a long illness, the situation often becomes temporarily a normal way of life. If the loved one is being cared for at home, the daily routine of assistance and medication becomes an accepted part of life; if he or she is in a hospice, the daily visits and the carrying out of minor personal tasks for the patient again become the norm. Grieving can be spread over the period of illness, consequently, there is time to laugh as well as cry.

## Other Negative Reactions

If a sympathizer has not experienced bereavement, then unrealistic expectations can lead to a lack of understanding, resulting in such unhelpful and sometimes less than considerate comments as: 'I know how you must be feeling.' How can they possibly know? It is not one of their family who has just passed away. 'Try to snap out of it,' they may say, implying unreasonable feelings of self-pity on the part of the bereaved. 'Time will heal', or, 'You *will* get over it', are probably the most inane of utterances. In the case of the recently disabled such comments as 'It might have been worse', or 'Thank God you still have the other one', are just numbing.

Possibly one on the most unwittingly hurtful reactions is to avoid mentioning the name of a lost loved one, and to quickly change the subject if any reference is made, as though that person had never lived. While this may be the result of not wishing to upset the bereaved, the sympathizer should realize that there is probably very little else that the bereaved person wishes to talk about, and he or she is probably thinking about nothing else, in any case.

Conversely, some bereaved people may not wish to talk openly about their loss, and this reasoned choice may be upset by someone of the view that feelings are best brought out into the open and got off one's chest. The bereaved would be wise in this case to avoid such a person, even if it means putting an old friendship at risk. The bereaved must be allowed to set his or her own pace and not become a victim of the dictates of others.

Bereavement can be quite a testing ground for friendships. While some will pass the test with flying colours, others may show a side never hitherto suspected, and they may exacerbate the pain of bereavement. Much distress can be caused by relying on someone such as this as an emotional prop. The breaking of a confidence probably ranks as one of the more unpleasant acts. Such a betrayal will obviously add to the bereaved's feelings of despair and desolation.


## EXPECTATIONS UPON BEREAVEMENT
### An Extreme Case

There cannot be a better illustration of others' negative and stereotyped reactions to bereavement than in the celebrated case of Lindy and Michael Chamberlain, whose baby daughter, Azaria, disappeared at Ayers Rock in Australia.

The two Seventh-day Adventists were on a family holiday with their three children aged six years, four years and ten weeks, and had pitched their camp like many adventurous Australians, near the Rock. The baby suddenly disappeared;

14

both parents stated that the child had been abducted by a wild dingo. At first their story was accepted – with some reluctance – by the Australian public; but the parents' reaction to the tragedy, their matter-of-fact explanation and their seemingly detached, unemotional attitude aroused much suspicion and eventually hostility. It was considered unacceptable for parents to behave in such a manner – there must be something more to the matter. The Chamberlains explained that their deep religious faith gave them the fortitude to bear their tragic loss, but this was far from acceptable to a society which expected a minimum show of grief. Alternative theories about the baby's disappearance began to circulate. The Chamberlains' attitude began to be seen as sinister; the idea of a dingo taking a baby away in its mouth was absurd; they must be lying – they must have wanted the child to die. The combination of what people regarded as eccentric religious views together with the location – the mysterious Ayers Rock – was basis enough for all kinds of bizarre allegations.

Most of the venom was directed at Lindy Chamberlain; she seemed altogether too cool, calm and collected to fit the popular image of a bereaved mother. Public hostility quickly took root, fed by countless media investigations. In the eyes of many she was as good as guilty of murder – only the due process of law and the sentence needed to be carried out. The State reluctantly found itself having to act by sheer force of public pressure. Both parents were indicted and convicted of murder, though the verdict as eventually overturned after the forensic evidence that had led to their conviction was totally discredited in an appeal court.

It is hard to comprehend the sheer hatred that was generated against the Chamberlains – especially Lindy. No one could offer any logical reason why she should wish to kill her child in such circumstances, and none was ever established. Yet, despite the Chamberlains' innocence having been established in a court of law, many still remain convinced of their guilt. Theirs is an extreme case of what can happen if certain expectations of grief behaviour are not fulfilled.

# 3 Grieving and the Help of Friends

## THE EXPERIENCE OF GRIEVING

Western society has sanitized the process of bereavement. In part, this is a good thing – professionalism at a very important time reduces to a minimum the chances of anything going wrong during the period when farewells are said. However, this is not only confined to the arrangements for the funeral. The need to sanitize one's grief for the benefit of other people is often an unspoken expectation. The British tradition of keeping a stiff upper lip does not allow the kind of open display of grief prevalent, for example, at middle-eastern funerals; such lack of restraint usually provokes acute embarrassment and discomfort in Westerners. The feeling, therefore, that a process of highly charged grieving is something almost to be ashamed of permeates most levels of our society. It is all right to indulge one's feelings within limits, at first, but the stiff upper lip philosophy is really the thing to observe, it is usually thought.

And yet, grieving is a necessity; it is the unavoidable means by which the mind and body are able to adjust to an immense change. It is difficult to appreciate it at the time, but we *need* to grieve. Death means *having* to forge a new life without the loved one, so painfully missed. The grieving process helps us, in time, to come to terms with our loss. People grieve in different ways. There are recognized aspects of grief, but the intensity, how they combine and in what order they appear, will be different for each person.

## Disbelief

Many people upon hearing the devastating news of their loved

16

one's death react with disbelief: the idea is preposterous – 'How can he have died?' 'How can she not be coming back to the house we have shared for so many years?'

We all are aware of our own mortality throughout our lives. For example, we make pension provisions for when we are older, knowing that our ability to work will diminish. We may occasionally think of how life will be at a much later stage in our lives. We know our life will end at some time in the future, but that inevitable end is forever being pushed back. However, the realization of our own temporary membership of humanity brutally confronts us upon hearing of the death of someone close to us. It is scarcely surprising that we retreat into disbelief – although we know death will happen to us and to the ones we love, at some time, now surely cannot be the time for it to happen.

It may be thought that the reality of seeing a deceased loved one will bring with it the realization that he or she will no longer be able to share our life. Logic should tell us this. But logic has no place here. Faced with the loss of so close a person, it is surely utterly reasonable to want to deny their death, at first. There *is* belief but it may only be belief *in part*.

That person has now died; they are not going to rejoin us after a little while. But their presence may still be felt. It may still feel as if they had never left. There is partial denial. Many small things can act as reminders of such a presence. The least object can take on deep significance. Being in a particular place or in a particular room, perhaps at a particular time, can make one feel as if that other person had never left, or that maybe time will see their safe return. There can be many sorts of reminders, from the most unlikely sources.

A widow in her mid-fifties said she never realized throughout her entire married life that her husband continually sniffed. One morning, the plumbing system developed an intermittent hissing noise, which brought to her attention for the first time an awareness of her late husband's habit. Even when the system had been rectified, his presence at a particular time every morning seemed almost tangible. She hoped he would be there, ready to emerge and call out 'What's for breakfast, darling?'

A few tissues quickly stuffed into a middle-aged man's hand by his terminally ill wife during her final stay in hospital, took on a deep significance after she had died. He had had a cold, and she had been concerned for his well-being. The tissues, unused, had been put away in a drawer with little more than a second thought, but they became intensely symbolic, when rediscovered after her death, of the care and concern she had always shown him during her lifetime.

To want to keep those we have known and loved is the most natural thing in the world. Such denial may be the body's way of cushioning emotions and preparing one to accept gradually what has happened.

Such feelings of initial denial are most likely to be expressed in the keeping of certain items of clothing. A familiar coat or hat or similar object may be left where it has always been. Any tendency on the part of others to recoil at this should be ignored. After all, such objects did no harm to anyone during a loved one's lifetime, so what possible physical or emotional harm can they do now? No one would suggest that a set of DIY tools, for example, should be banished from a home just because the owner has died. They are likely to remain and to be used in the same environment, the only difference being that another pair of hands will operate them. If familiar objects comfort a bereaved person, then they are justified. It becomes a matter for concern only when there is a long-term, obsessive clinging to anything and everything that belonged to a lost loved one.

## Anger

To someone experiencing grief for the first time, anger is perhaps the least expected feeling. But it is often a necessary emotion in order to release the inner pressure that has built up. Anger may be directed towards someone or something in particular, or it may be unfocused.

The medical profession is probably well used to hearing the

anger of distraught relatives, some of which may be directed at them – anger at whether enough was done by surgeons – whether or not the patient received the best possible care and skill – whether more of something might have saved them. Such reactions are not unusual. We have placed the life of the one we loved into the hands of complete strangers and it would seem they have let us down. One young man was so angry with the medical profession that his announcement of his father's death in the newspaper included the words 'With no thanks to the surgeons involved'. He admitted, however, in retrospect, that his father had received excellent care, but he simply could not appreciate it at the time. He needed to vent his anger. He needed someone to blame and the obvious choice was the hospital.

A common recipient of anger is God. He is, after all, the one whom we have been led to believe loves us and cares for us, and here he is allowing our loved one to die. A thirty-five year-old man was so distressed when he was told that his mother had only another three months to live that he rushed out of the hospital, climbed into his car and just drove. He had no idea of where he was going. He desperately needed a private, enclosed space in which he could give vent to his feelings of anger and outrage *at God.* He used every profanity he could think of in an attempt to hurt and be revenged on God. After half an hour of this behaviour he parked his car and went to sleep. When he awoke he felt slightly foolish. Whether what he had done was the right or wrong thing he did not know, but he felt better and more able to face his tragedy.

Anger may also be directed at oneself, the bereaved. By tracing the pattern of events leading to a death, it may be felt that if only one had done more at a particular stage, death need not have been the outcome: 'Why didn't I realize he was so ill and insist that he saw the doctor, instead of letting him fob me off with reassurances that it would pass?'

This is an echo of regret shared by many. One middle-aged widow was so overcome with self-anger that she regarded a coincidental illness suffered shortly after her husband's death, which left her with a minor handicap, as just recompense for not having taken action sooner, thereby averting her tragic loss.

The gap left by a loved one may be so large that resentment may be felt towards the deceased for having left. This may be a corollary to disbelief – have they really gone, or could they return if they so wished and provide relief from all the unnecessary distress?

'We were doing so well together; we had everything to live for and we were beginning to enjoy the fruits of our hard work. Now this! The plans I had for both of us are in ruins. I feel as though he did it almost deliberately, just to hurt me.'

The harsh practicalities of everyday life continue whether or not the loved one is still present. Bills still have to be paid, repairs still have to be carried out to property, and so on, entailing expenditure of physical effort and money. It is sometimes the case that the loved one may not have been particularly prudent in financial matters. Inadequate life insurance may leave a widow in substantially reduced circumstances. She may have to find a job to supplement her modified income. If she lacks certain skills, this may mean training or retraining. A widower may have to seek care for his children, and nurseries and child-minders do not operate seven days a week and twenty-four hours a day. A completely different way of life may have to be adopted. In some households it is the man who manages the financial side of matters. In these days of sex equality this may seem quite preposterous, but many older couples still regard the finances as being the man's job. Consequently, appalling ignorance on the part of a widow – perhaps through no fault of her own – may leave her bewildered, unable to cope, and angry with her husband for leaving her so unprepared.

Anger need not be directed at an identifiable person or group. It may be directed at the world in general:

'I see everyone enjoying themselves; but they don't give a fig about me. I went shopping the other day; I hate shopping. There was this woman and she bumped into my trolley quite by accident. She looked annoyed, as if it was my fault – it was nothing really. But that was enough! I yelled at her not to be so bloody clumsy! I needed to scream at someone and she was just perfect. I suppose I must have been hoping she would start to fight back so I could let off more steam. She didn't, though; she seemed dazed at my outburst and just let me shout at her.'

Anger can turn into bitterness. There may be the feeling of being victimized by an unseen force, leading to such attitudes as:

'Why couldn't it have happened to him and his kids? He's got plenty of money to compensate him. What have I got left? He can get drunk whenever and wherever he likes to drown his sorrows. I've just got to keep on working when it all seems so pointless.'

This was the reaction of a divorced man in his middle-thirties who had lost his only daughter in a car accident. He felt embarrassed when recalling his feelings, but admitted that he had meant every word of it at the time. It bothered him for a long time, though, that he had felt so bitter and angry. His eventual realization that, for him, this was a necessary release on his journey through bereavement, did much to unburden his conscience.

However, anger that cannot be relieved by normal displays of emotion may be a cause for concern. When it builds up inside and cannot be assuaged, clinical depression could result. It cannot be stated too strongly that help should be sought in a situation such as this, either from one's GP or from bereavement counselling.

## Guilt

Bereaved persons very often experience feelings of guilt. Although individuals are likely to perceive such feelings as being unique to him or herself, in fact they signal a loving relationship, and have a multiplicity of causes.

An inclination to blame oneself for not having done this or that emerges in tragic situations where it is usually the case that nothing else could have been done. That is not sufficient, however, for the survivor. He or she may regard it as an indication of hypocrisy, perhaps even an insult to the memory of the lost loved one, to accept that no more could have been done. Such acceptance seems improper; therefore blame *must* be attached to the bereaved, to themselves by themselves. They feel partially responsible. The death itself is the evidence of their guilt.

Guilt may be prevalent for a variety of reasons. For example, one may have reached the conclusion that there was a pattern of events leading to a death. This may bring with it the idea that if there had been intervention at a particular stage, death might have been averted:

'I should have sought a second opinion, immediately, instead of meekly accepting our GP's verdict when she first felt unwell. It seemed like a normal headache which went away again. If only I'd acted sooner none of this would have happened.'

If one was truly responsible for contributing towards the death of a loved one in such circumstances then, by implication, the deceased must have had, at best, only limited responsibility for his or her own life. This, evidently, cannot be the case. The pattern of events, therefore, must also be seen from the perspective of the deceased. Were they secretive about their state of health? Did they know something was wrong but refuse to tell anyone? Could they not have exercised more care – were they really rather reckless? Didn't they know it was dangerous to carry on in such a way? They are likely to have had a large measure of control over their own lives and if guilt *has* to be apportioned then it cannot be confined to the bereaved person alone.

Feelings of guilt over not having said goodbye or sorry are very common. Missing a hospital visit on the very evening the loved one died is an example, but the list is endless, and even if one guilty feeling is appeased the chances are another will surface. Regardless of the cause, it must be borne in mind that whatever a bereaved person thinks they may have done or should have done, it can have had no bearing on the death of the loved one. Even hoping someone would die to end their pain and suffering will not have brought about that person's death – his or her life took its course, and no amount of guilt and regret is going to alter that. It is not possible to wish somebody dead. Trying to imagine life without someone, even occasionally thinking that life might be more tolerable without, for example, the burden of a terminally-ill loved one, cannot have the effect of hastening that person's death. Although feelings of guilt are quite understandable in such a situation, they must be seen for what they really are – a response to a tragic situation.

The death of a young person can sometimes bring out feelings of guilt in those who are much older: 'I've already had a good innings – she was so young and had so much to live for. It should have been me.' This view of life would seem to indicate that there is a natural order which has temporarily gone wrong, and that one should feel guilty for upsetting this pre-ordained system. Of course, there is no such thing. None of us has any control over how events will take shape. We are all a part of nature and the way it operates is a mystery to us. An older person who feels that a young person's demise is somehow a question of morality must have an exceedingly complicated philosophy.

A death can often bring with it a degree of financial stability. Where there may have been an element of struggling before with such things as mortgages and HP settlements there may now be full property ownership, a pension and life assurance policies to ease the financial burden. This, too, can bring its own form of guilt:

'I know we talked about getting each other insured in case one of us should die, but it was just one of those things that you do. I never dreamed for one moment just what it would mean in reality. I am fit and able to work but have no need to – at least, not just for the money. I've never been so well off. This cannot be right. I'm only in this position because of my terrible loss; I feel awful.'

This reaction is understandable, but it is far removed from what the lost loved one surely intended. Such provision is an expression of a loving relationship, financial hardship would certainly not have been the loved one's wish. A new life is going to have to be carved out, and financial independence is the tool which the lost loved one has personally provided to enable the survivor to carry on.

## Fear

Fear and worry after a bereavement are only to be expected. The life that lies ahead no longer includes the support, hopes and aspirations of the one lost. Now decisions must be made alone, albeit with the help of friends and family. The future may appear uncertain and frightening.

The bereaved may wonder how coping is going to be possible. Most relationships work on a division of labour principle which has probably emerged over a number of years. That division can no longer operate. Everyday tasks that were undertaken by other hands will now have to be learned. The fear of being unable to cope, though, is often transient. In time it will be discovered that nothing so stimulates the acquisition of new skills as sheer necessity. Many people ask themselves why they never got to grips before with such simple things as changing a plug, mending a fuse, or operating the washing machine.

It is not uncommon for the bereaved to fear that a similar tragedy is shortly to befall themselves. A pattern of events is seen as having been set in motion, and it is regarded as only a matter of time before that pattern is complete.

## A Case History: Kit

Kit, aged thirty-two, lost both his parents within days of each other. Both had had terminal illnesses, with identical symptoms. The double tragedy convinced him that the illness must be hereditary, and that he would shortly join his mother and father. The slightest deviation from his normal pattern of health caused him the greatest concern.

One day he could stand it no longer. He decided to commit all his fears to paper, and to try to deal logically with them. He attempted to trace the origins of his father's illness. It may have begun three and a half years previously. The symptoms his father had experienced had seemed insignificant at first. The usual patent medicines were taken in the hope of curing the problem, but were ineffectual. His mother had urged his father to seek medical advice but he ignored her pleas, stubbornly refusing to let what he termed a minor complaint interrupt his career. He eventually had an emergency operation for cancer. The delay of nearly a year before seeking medical advice, Kit reasoned, had contributed to his father's demise.

He considered that the origins of his mother's illness lay in severe worry and stress. She had been a nurse, and he felt she must have been aware of the danger his father was running, though he knew there was nothing more she could have done to alter her husband's stubborn refusal to seek early medical attention. He felt she must have kept her anxiety bottled up to the point where she, too, succumbed to what he saw as a stress-related condition. He finally concluded that his parents' deaths were a tragic coincidence, and that hereditary illness was unlikely; in any case, his parents could not possibly have been blood relatives. Far from his own demise being imminent, the laws of probability would seem to indicate otherwise: for a whole family to suffer the same fate from unrelated origins must surely be considered a million-to-one chance.

The loss of a child may make one over-protective towards the remaining child or children, for fear that they are vulnerable because of what has happened. However, the possibility of the same tragedy recurring in the same family, especially where the time scale is so short, must be remote.

A feeling of isolation can, understandably, induce feelings of fear and anxiety. It may not happen immediately, though. Comprehension of all that one's loss entails may not be complete for some little while. The final realization of a permanent loss, though, and its attendant feelings of loneliness and vulnerability, is the point at which defeating, or being defeated

25

by fear itself is going to have to be faced. For most people this is something they *will* be able to handle but it does take time and patience. It will not necessarily be an easy process. It will require fortitude. At times fear may give way to intense anger directed at oneself, at the deceased, or at the world in general. Facing reality and coming to terms with it *will* be achieved, however.

## Hallucinations

Hallucinations are by no means uncommon, especially during the early days of bereavement: 'Several times I "saw" my husband, quite clearly. I can still describe the clothes he was wearing. It does not happen now, though.'

Not only may the bereaved believe they have seen their lost loved ones they may hear their voices or experience their presence in other ways. It is something which is rarely talked about for fear of ridicule or worse. Such hallucinations, though, can be comforting, and those who have experienced them say they ease the path of grief. Hallucinations are mostly experienced by older people who have been in a loving relationship for a number of years.

## Sadness

Sadness can arise without any warning whatsoever. The smallest glimpse or sound can revive floods of memories which reach the point where they become almost overwhelming. It can happen anywhere, at any time, and attempting to explain one's feelings to others who may be present can seem impossibly complicated, even assuming there is anyone with the time to listen and understand.

Such feelings will be very common during the early stages of bereavement. They may well continue, though at infrequent intervals, for the rest of one's life – they are, after all, a comfort and a tribute to the memory of a lost loved one.

It is important to give way to these feelings and not to be constrained by the feeling that one must be 'strong'. Releasing feelings of sadness has a necessary emotional purpose, and attempting to suppress them might well lead to problems in other areas, such as unpleasant physical symptoms. The need to release sadness will not diminish: denying it and being 'strong' simply delays the healing process.

# BREAKING BAD NEWS

Informing someone of the loss of their loved one is an immense responsibility. Feelings of apprehension about the response of the bereaved person, and about one's ability to cope with that reaction, are understandable. One might even be fearful that one is going to be blamed for bringing the bad news.

Very often this task is undertaken by the medical profession or the police; however, there may be a tendency for it to be seen as part of the job and it may be left to the individual's discretion as to how the news is broken. The aftermath of the shock is then left to those accompanying the bereaved person to deal with as best they can.

To the medical profession, letting kin know of the death of a loved one can perhaps become rather routine. A degree of insensitivity, even callousness, can sometimes creep in. It is a sad fact that there is a woeful lack of education in this field. Representatives of organizations dealing with the terminally ill will probably visit medical and nursing students for the odd day or half-day during training, but this cannot be described as educative; these are talks which inform but do not train. Breaking bad news is a task which needs a great deal of compassion. Perhaps all hospitals will become enlightened enough to realize this in time, and to treat it as an area of specialization. Fortunately, the beginnings of progress in this direction are in evidence.

## A Strategy for Breaking Bad News

The Gale Centre for Creative Therapy, at Loughton, Essex, has devised a short guide to the breaking of bad news and I am grateful for their permission to quote from it:

27

'The process of implying by your behaviour that you are going to break some bad news usually strengthens the listener and gives them a few moments to prepare themselves. So it can be very helpful to say, "I think you need to prepare yourself for some bad news", or, "I have some bad news to tell you".

'Often this encounter will be on a doorstep or in a busy casualty department, so it is best to find a better place to break the actual news and your next line could be, "Could I come in?" or "Please would you come with me". If you are on your own territory, as in a hospital, you can take the person to a quiet place that you have prepared and tell them the news there. The news may need to be broken urgently, but a couple of minutes spent preparing will make it much easier for you and the bereaved person.

*'Now you will have to work out in your own mind how you will cope with the reaction.*

'It is generally accepted that the person breaking the bad news should stay with the bereaved person for a little while and at least until someone else is able to come to be with them. It can be helpful to hold a hand, or, if someone is very tearful, to put an arm around them.

'Whatever the reaction you receive it is likely to be a powerful one and you will have to be ready in yourself to cope with any combination of tears, silence, screaming and violent disbelief. The best way to cope with all of these is to remain calm.

'In the case of violent emotions they don't normally last long and it is generally your fear of the strength of the emotion and your inability to control it which will unsettle you. Remember that the news you have just broken is so terrible that shouting, screaming and running away are normal ways of coping. You should do your best to make sure the person doesn't hurt themself and you may need to physically restrain them, providing you do not get hurt yourself. Remember that you are only responsible for breaking the bad news. You have not caused it and don't have to feel guilty about it.

28

'If the bereaved person cries you may be able to comfort them with an arm around the shoulder or by holding a hand. Where somebody goes silent, it is probably best to remain in contact with them by occasionally asking them if they are all right and just sitting with them holding their hand. In all cases your job is to be supportive and the best way to do this is to say and do only as much as is necessary until you are prompted by the words or actions of the bereaved person. After some minutes you will also have to help them to deal with practicalities, like calling in other relatives or neighbours, or collecting children from school.

'There is often a temptation on the part of the carer to fill the silence or say something. This should be avoided, listening and saying what is necessary when it is necessary is the important thing. If you are caring and sympathetic to the bereaved person you will be more likely to get it right for yourself and for them. Once a friend or relative has arrived you can leave, providing that you are no longer needed. At this stage there may be a temptation to stay longer than is really necessary.'

## FRIENDS

No one can pretend that helping a recently bereaved person through their pain is a straightforward task. Indeed, some bereaved persons may prefer to come to terms with their grief in their own way, by excluding others from their pain, thereby undertaking what they see as a process of self-healing. Self-healing does indeed have a major role to play, but supportive and understanding friends are of inestimable value, even if at the time it is difficult to appreciate fully the contribution they can make. Many people consider members of their own family to be their closest friends, but if a deep loss affects them as well, their ability to help may be reduced. A friend outside the family circle is often very important, therefore. It may even be necessary to seek a new friendship for the purpose of helping one through grief. Do let those around you know, if this is the case. No one can offer care and understanding unless they know you want it. Enlightened general practitioners can be a starting point in finding the kind of person who is right for your needs. However, do not just accept the first person who comes along. It is important that he or she is in tune with you, and only you will know that.

## A Good Listener

A person who is good at listening is essential when one just needs to talk. 'I found few people willing or able to listen to me and yet that was the only thing I needed; just someone to listen.' This was the lament of a young lady who had lost her father a year previously. She hadn't a close friend in whom she could confide and no one had thought of helping her to find one.

What makes a good listener? Many people have the ability to listen, but their reactions are not necessarily positive or helpful. Two people engaged in general conversation will both probably give the impression of listening intently to the other's point of view. Yet it is quite possible for each to be on a completely different wavelength, and though they seem to be listening to each other, they may simply be pausing for breath whilst formulating the next part of their contribution to the debate, and actually paying minimal attention to what the other person is saying.

Ideally, a good listener for the bereaved should possess *empathy* – the ability to project oneself into another's situation and to understand another's feelings. Local branches of self-help groups are excellent for establishing such contacts. However, because someone has personal experience of bereavement, it does not automatically make him or her empathetic. Some may think they are when they are simply good at being a shoulder to cry on. They remain detached, and while they may be able to sympathize they cannot take their emotions a stage further by 'sharing' the experience of the newly bereaved.

An empathetic person will strive to make you feel comfortable, and accept your tears without attempting to help you over those tears quickly. He or she will know that grown men do (and should) cry. The bereaved will be encouraged to feel less inhibited and more relaxed, free from the worry of having to edit their feelings. Empathetic people will not counter your expressions of grief with constant references to their own experiences; they will listen intently and not put their own interpretation upon what you are saying.

Such friends – perhaps they ought to be called 'healers' – will recognize that the pace of healing can only be determined by the strengths of the one who is grieving, and will have patience if the healing process takes longer than they may, at first, have expected. They will know that their task is to be led by their bereaved charge, not to try to take the lead themselves. They will try, too, to instil patience in their charge if the road to recovery seems long. Above all, they know there is no formula for reaching the end of grief.

The good listener does not proffer advice, or make judgements. He or she should be a guide rather than a factotum, especially where practicalities are concerned. It is important that the bereaved be encouraged to do things for themselves, where possible, and not become unnecessarily dependent upon others, the exception being during the initial and most painful period of grief.

Such a healer will be aware of the bereaved's need to release the inner pain that has been maturing during the period of bereavement, and will nurture it with gentleness and understanding. They will not keep saying how sorry they are for the loss; in fact, they will be careful to avoid saying this at all after the initial condolences.

It must be remembered, though, that such healers, such emotional caregivers, are as human as everyone else. They may not always feel comfortable with some of the things that are said. They will probably have had upsets and crises of their own and must be forgiven if they occasionally appear less than responsive to the bereaved's demands. If mild impatience should arise, especially during the later stages of bereavement, it may even have a beneficial effect on the bereaved, though this should be a transient feeling, easily forgotten, and not something which threatens to develop into conflict.

Such friends will regard the time spent with you as being *your* time. They will not make you feel that you are encroaching on time which they can ill-afford or which they grudge. They will not expect to be rewarded with constant expressions of gratitude. (You will, of course, feel grateful, but they will realize that you will express your gratitude in your own good time.) Their concern is to assist you on your road to recovery.

## Practical Help

The routine tasks of everyday life do not come to a standstill during bereavement. They can, however, easily be forgotten. They may appear burdensome, pointless, a total waste of time in the light of the loss suffered. Humdrum tasks such as vacuum cleaning and washing dishes may well go by the board.

Many people are only too willing to do the odd task for a friend suffering the loss of a loved one – the occasional shopping or baking, for instance. It is a help to the bereaved person; it is also satisfying to the person who is offering the help. It takes a very different kind of person, however, to offer ongoing help with everyday tasks for as long as is necessary. To be prepared to become involved in such a way and to offer oneself as an unpaid Samaritan requires a much deeper commitment than that offered by the casual 'If there is anything I can do, just let me know' kind. These people can also be of value, but in a limited way, and in a way which is often only convenient to them.

Listening to the bereaved and hearing from them which tasks need performing should be the caregivers' concern, and they should be prepared to adapt themselves accordingly, helping with practical jobs such as housework, errands, taking the children to school, delivering letters and so on. They will probably help with planning the diary – appointments can easily be forgotten at such a time, and there are so many –

32

but they should never seek to take over the bereaved's life. One's natural inclination to do as much as possible should not render the bereaved helpless without one's help. Important though such total support might be in the early stages of bereavement, the realization of a bereaved person's need to return to self-reliance in the longer term is essential.

Practical help extends to welcoming the bereaved into one's home, but not to insisting that they stay or spend an evening there – their privacy must be respected.

It cannot be stressed too strongly that undertaking the task of helping a recently bereaved person is *not* a decision to be entered into lightly. Feeling under pressure to do so either through a natural desire to help, or because one feels one is the 'obvious' choice, is a totally inadequate reason for embarking upon a major responsibility. Once started, the process cannot be easily reversed, and indeed trying to do so can cause far more hurt to the bereaved person than if they had not been offered help at all. It is a time-consuming activity, and therefore time must be available to be freely given. Trying to be a good Samaritan whilst being over-committed on other fronts is as unfair to the bereaved person as it is to one's other responsibilities.

It must be said, too, that bereaved people should avoid those do-gooders who like to feel they have a social conscience, and like to be seen to be offering help. Such people are likely to be domineering and will only offer help on *their* terms. The bereaved is a mere catalyst for their activities and a prop to their own self-esteem. The Oxford English Dictionary defines help thus: 'To provide [a person] with means towards what is needed or sought; be of use or service to [a person].' Self-interest is not in it.

# 4  Caring for Those Who are Dying

Many people will realize that they are going to lose a loved one because of an incurable illness. Being told – it is hoped with sensitivity – that someone close is to die may well cause grief to begin long before the experience of bereavement takes place. Grief will only occur, though, where there is acceptance that what is going to happen is inevitable. Receiving such tragic news will not, in itself, mean acceptance of impending bereavement. Acceptance happens only when there is a realization that no more can be done to preserve the life of the loved one beyond the period remaining.

The first reaction will quite possibly be one of denial, which will only disappear when all possible avenues of salvation have been exhausted, such as seeking further medical advice. There may subsequently be a variety of emotions – anger, guilt, bargaining ('Please let him have his birthday, first'), sadness, acceptance. Such emotions do not necessarily follow any pattern; they may be mutually exclusive or they may be present in different combinations and to different degrees.

It may be felt, at first, that nothing positive or good can emerge from such a tragic situation. Eventually, though, there will probably be a realization that this is one of the most significant periods in the relationship, because of one precious quality: time

## TO TELL OR NOT TO TELL

So far, the prospect of losing a loved one has been considered from the perspective of those who are to become bereaved. But what of those who have only a short while to live?

34

Should they be told? This is a question which has no definitive answer, but enlightened opinion would seem to be in favour of the dying knowing or, at least, having an awareness of their situation. Historically, the medical profession has conveyed the impression that to let a patient know he or she is dying is somehow the equivalent of failure or a betrayal of trust. Their task, as they have seen it, is to preserve life, not to preside over it. Despite this, serious consideration ought to be given to the question of allowing a dying person the chance (some may call it the right) to grieve for her or himself, and to grieve for those they will be leaving behind. The alternative is to avoid giving direct answers to the loved one about the prospects of recovery, thereby possibly denying him or her such an opportunity.

The dying do not suddenly become gullible just because they are dying. Indeed, it could be argued that their powers of perception are greatly enhanced. For example, they will be acutely aware of their surroundings and of the type of care being offered to them, and refusal to confirm or deny their suspicions will exacerbate their emotional pain, and lead to fear, anger, even depression.

These feelings may not necessarily be brought to the surface, but they could well heighten the agony of not knowing the truth. In such circumstances, though, the dying may feel they owe a duty of consideration towards those close to them and, accordingly, refrain from asking questions. It could be argued that by not being told, they are being denied a degree of control over their own lives; knowing the truth can help a dying person to prepare, and may fulfil a long-felt *need* for preparation.

In any given situation there will be criteria which dictate the course to take. Generally, however, most people *will* wish to know that they have only a little time left. Denying a dying loved one such honesty may be a decision later regretted. Communication should be undertaken by a person who is very well acquainted with the dying loved one. The one thing that must be allowed for is time: time for the news to be absorbed and understood, and time to deal with the reaction to the news. This may be one of complete acceptance

35

or it may be something utterly unpredictable. In any event, time and support are essential. Many will wish to know how much time they have remaining, but Elizabeth Kubler-Ross suggests in *On Death and Dying* that taking away hope from the dying by prescribing the *exact* amount of time remaining is little better than telling them that their condition will end their life at some stage and saying no more. Letting someone know there is a minimum and a maximum amount of time remaining is to be honest as well as providing a degree of hope.

Some people however, may need to cling to the hope of life. The knowledge that they will never recover may lead to hopelessness, perhaps even desperation, and a feeling of isolation from their loved ones. They may reject the news that they are incurably ill, steadfastly refusing to countenance any possibility other than that of recovery. In the early stages especially, this may be accompanied by a refusal to accept any help that might be construed as relating to the care of a dying person. During the later stages, rejection of such help may not be possible, but the necessity of having such help administered may be received with great distress. To be with someone in this situation, seeing them making plans for a future that can never be fulfilled and to watch them withdraw into themselves, can be heartbreaking. Those who are able to accept the inevitability of their dying can not only grieve for themselves, they can perhaps help and prepare those around them to grieve as well.

There will be some situations where a choice will not be possible; for example, where a person is too ill or is unconscious. But the decision to be open and honest, where this is possible, is one that should not be rejected because of the finality and the seeming brutality of the message. Its effect on the dying loved one must of course be weighed up with great consideration and compassion, but it is probable that not concealing the truth will prove to be the start of a new beginning; a period of time in which much can be said and done; a period in which easing the path of grief for everyone can commence.

Conversely, it may be the dying who are the first to know. The burden of deciding when and how the news should be broken to their loved ones may fall upon their shoulders. There may be a little time in which to prepare themselves and to assess their own feelings; they may wish not to let their loved ones know immediately. They will, of course, have to know at some time, but it will take courage to tell them, and there will probably be a great deal of concern as to how the news will be received.

Where time permits, preparation is essential and good counsellors will be only too willing to give all the help that is needed. Where circumstances allow and where courage permits, the news may well be broken by the dying loved one, personally, perhaps with the aid of a counsellor. To have the news broken only by an outsider, especially where the outsider sees it as just a part of his or her job, may well create additional distress.

Finally, it is as well to reflect on what dying actually is. Do we not all begin the process of dying from the moment we are born? In this context, the difference between those who are terminally ill and those who are not is that the former have received some indication of the extent to which their lives remain; the latter have not. It is by no means uncommon for the terminally ill to outlive those who have not been so diagnosed.

## A Case History: Bill and Edith

Bill and Edith had been married for over twenty-five years and had enjoyed good health for most of that time. They had taken each other for granted on occasions – nothing unusual in a married relationship – but were happy and well suited. Fairly early on in their relationship they had discussed how they would react should either of them fall seriously ill, and had decided their love was strong enough to overcome any difficulties. As their married life progressed their mutual reassurances on this subject developed into something more serious. As a result, they made a pact: they promised always to be completely honest with each other if either were to become terminally ill.

The test came much sooner than expected. Edith became seriously ill and her condition was diagnosed as terminal. Only Bill was told of the terrible news; the pact they had made with each other occupied his thoughts for days. He searched his conscience trying to reach a decision as to whether or how and when he should tell her. Sadly for Bill, his courage failed him. He felt he could not take away from Edith the one thing that he thought she needed: hope. Take that away, he reasoned, and she would have nothing left.

Edith, however, was more aware of her situation than Bill realized. Not satisfied with his bland reassurances as to her recovery, she secretly found out the truth from another source, but her desire to protect Bill led *her* to keep the fact that she knew the truth from *him*.

Bill lost Edith without their ever having talked to each other about her impending death; he now feels profound regret at his decision not to have shared his knowledge with her, especially since he learned a little while after her death that she had sought the confidence of another. He feels that not taking the opportunity to grieve together or say goodbye while they had the chance, has added to his loss.

## WHERE AND HOW SHOULD SOMEONE DIE?

At the beginning of the century most people died where they had lived for most of their lives. They died in familiar surroundings, surrounded by those with whom they had shared life. Today, we have been educated into accepting that most deaths occur away from home. The home is for living in, not for dying in. Similarly, today, the home is regarded by many as being not a proper place in which to introduce life.

This view is beginning to change, however. It could be argued that, with exceptions, the terminally ill need not necessarily be seen as ill in the accepted sense of the word. In medical terms, there is now no more help for them. They may be receiving medication and need help with bodily functions, but there is much that can be done for them in order to make the time remaining to them as pleasant and as *joyful* as possible, and to allow the concept of illness to be put to one side for a while.

The ability to cope with the dying by those nearest to them depends not only on the people themselves, of course, but on

38

practical considerations. If the home is not practicable then the terminally ill must be either in hospital or in a hospice.

# HOSPITAL

The hospital's function is to treat illnesses and eventually to discharge their patients. No one wishes to remain in hospital for longer than necessary; we may fall in love with our nurses; we may find new friends; we may discover things about ourselves which we had hitherto never realized; but our return home, recovered, is awaited with eager anticipation. There is a desire to return to the normal patterns of life, to rejoin our family, friends and colleagues.

For those who have no prospect of recovering and whose future is now circumscribed, the situation is different. Remaining in hospital is unquestionably essential if there are emergency problems to be treated. Many terminally ill people, however, are not in any immediate need of hospital care, and would almost certainly prefer to be in their own home (with the necessary support) rather than in the clinical environment of a hospital.

The prospect of a dying loved one spending his or her remaining life in a hospital unless it is absolutely necessary, can be distressing both at the time and in retrospect. Home is the place where we can be ourselves; where we can relax and do things we would never dream of doing elsewhere. How much more important then, it must be for someone who is dying to be at home. If this is not possible, then those closest should be allowed to stay in hospital with the loved one for as long as is wished. Normal hospital rules should be relaxed as far as is possible so that the hospital room becomes an extension of the home, for the dying person.

## A Case History: Rebecca

Some fifteen years ago Rebecca, who was then fourteen, regularly visited her grandmother in the large geriatric ward in which she was being looked after. She had only weeks to live, and was there only for the purpose of being looked after; treatment was no longer possible. She confided in Rebecca that though she was afraid of the physical pain caused by her terminal cancer, she was even more afraid of the prospect of dying in hospital. Rebecca reflected that the things preventing her grandmother from returning home were twofold; firstly, a complete lack of understanding on the part of her family as to her emotional needs, and secondly, the problem of providing adequate help at home. Meekly accepting at the time that it was 'for the best', Rebecca nevertheless realized that this was what suited everybody except her poor grandma, the one who was dying and whose wishes should really have come first. Her grandmother did, indeed, die in hospital and Rebecca's grief was, she feels, exacerbated by this. Her sadness remains even to this day.

## HOME

The decision to care for a dying loved one at home is a loving, generous one. It will not be without difficulties, but the rewards will be immense, although perhaps not immediately obvious. However, there *will* be a realization that this was the best thing possible.

The path of the dying can be greatly eased by familiar surroundings and with their loved ones performing small practical tasks of everyday life for them. The loving caregiver will accept comments sbout how such acts of assistance should be performed without feeling there is a complaining attitude. Obviously, given the choice, the dying would prefer to do these things for themselves, and it is not unreasonable for them to try to guide the carer into thinking in an *empathetic* way. It also gives them a degree of control; after all, just because someone needs assistance with self-care tasks does not mean they have to lose their right to self-determination. Those who have the ability to control their lives *through their carers* can still claim to be independent.

The term 'carer' is a fairly new concept and those who perform this role are gradually being recognized for the highly valuable work they perform. A carer is at the forefront of a social service which extends outwards and involves many people. The first thing a carer must remember is not to be afraid to ask for help. Despite increasing recognition, it is all too easy to assume that, as the dying loved one is at home, all the responsibility must, therefore, fall on the carer's shoulders.Consequently, there is often a reluctance to seek out and request services to be brought into the home, as if this was somehow asking for charity. The provision of services in this situation is a right. If the period remaining for that loved one is to be made as meaningful as possible, then it is, in effect, *a duty* to ensure that maximum help is obtained. Of course, the provision and the adequacy of help may vary from area to area, but there are independent organizations which can offer advice.

## The General Practitioner

Good GPs are worth their weight in gold. Their concern will not begin and end at the bedside; they will ensure that a chain of support is set up. They will also have the foresight to ensure the well-being of the caregivers, realizing that if they become distraught and overworked, the position of the dying loved one will be at risk. If the carer shares the same GP as the dying one, it may be necessary to consider seeking another doctor for the time being. The needs of the carer may become overlooked if a GP has both as patients.

## The District Nurse

District nurses are hospital-trained nurses specializing in caring for people at home. They are employed by district health authorities. They will carry out specialist tasks such as giving injections. They can also assess the home environment and give advice on how to adapt it to cope with any special demands, in addition to advising on such problems as incontinence, or how

41

to lift someone with minimal wear and tear on the caregiver.

## Macmillan Nurses

Their concern is to improve the quality of life of cancer patients and their families, whether in hospital, in a hospice or at home. Their role in the home is to give as much support to the caregivers as possible; they can arrange regular visits at any time of the day or night, in order to ease the pressures of caring for the dying. They can also assist in the provision of a whole range of equipment.

## Domiciliary Home Care Teams

Some localities may have a scheme which aims to provide, in the home, the care which is provided in a hospice. The Macmillan organization or the Marie Curie Cancer Care organization may have such a scheme in one's area, and the GP will usually instigate a request for such help. The team will have certain criteria: to control pain and other symptoms, and to relieve the anxiety and fear these may produce; to advise, counsel and support patients and families so as to make the most of their strengths and improve their confidence and ability to cope; to help patients retain their independence so that they can remain in control of their own lives. This will mean responding quickly when help or equipment is needed, and providing back-up beds as a safety net should circumstances change.

Skilled teams have dramatically reduced the need for admission to a hospice, and many who do need temporary hospice care return home eventually.

## The Occupational Therapist

These are employed by or through the local Social Services department and will carry out assessments, advise on necessary adaptations to the home and arrange for such adaptations to be fitted. They are also trained in the correct way to handle and lift patients. Occupational therapists are also employed by the district health authorities, and they will provide the relevant specialist treatment associated with a medical diagnosis. This is arranged via the GP, specialist or consultant.

## Health Visitors and Health Care Workers

Health visitors are nurses who can provide information and advice on the availability of local services. They will be able to provide the necessary link between home and the Social Services department, and offer help with regard to benefits and other services that may be available, together with practical advice and support. They are also concerned with the emotional aspect of the situation, and are there for this purpose if the caregiver or the dying loved one so wishes.

Since April 1990, the local Social Services departments have introduced health care workers as part of their extended home nursing scheme.

## Social Workers

Social workers will advise on a range of practical and personal problems. Specialist social workers who are able to work with those with individual handicaps are also available from the local Social Services department.

## Continence Advisers

They are able to assess the problem and propose the relevant treatment; they are able to suggest ways of coping and can provide any special items of equipment needed; and they will be able to advise about the provision of a laundry service.

## The Home Care Service

The Home Care Service (formerly known as the Home Help Service until 1990) is a part of the local Social Services and is there to provide help according to the needs of each person.

The Home Care Manager will make an initial assessment and detail the kind of help that is available.

## Disabled Living Centres (for Aids & Adaptations)

These are organizations which deal with the problems of everyday living. They are either of charitable status or partly or wholly financed by the local Social Services. There is usually a wide range of equipment on display and advice and information is offered by qualified physiotherapists and occupational therapists. They provide an excellent way of actually seeing aids and adaptations in the sort of environment in which they will be used, making the installation of necessary equipment in the home appear more 'user friendly' when it is first put into operation. Disabled Living Centres have been in existence for some sixteen years and are spread across the United Kingdom and in many areas of the world. The Royal College of Physicians Report in 1986 recommended one per district. However, there are some areas of the country which are still without such a facility.

## The British Red Cross Society

This excellent organization has many branches around the country, some situated in or near hospitals and health centres. They can provide short-term loans of equipment such as wheelchairs, bed pans, crutches, etc. They also run short courses on the practical side of caring.

## Care Attendant Schemes

These services make an invaluable contribution towards easing the burden of the carer. Care attendants are trained and will carry out a variety of tasks that the caregiver would normally perform. The service comes under a variety of names, for example, the Crossroads Care Attendant Scheme, the Leonard Cheshire Family Support Service. Some are exclusively local whilst others are branches of national associations. They are excellent for giving the caregiver a break from time to time; or they can also become part of the home-care team.

## Sitting Services

These are run by voluntary groups in most areas. The participants are not trained in the usual sense of the word, but their experience is usually sound. They will provide a welcome break for the carer for a few hours.

## The Provision of Local Information

Areas vary in their provision of information services, and much can be missed by the person seeking information. It is therefore very important to locate a source which can give as much information as possible concerning relevant services and organizations. It is probably a good idea to start looking under 'Health', 'Disablement', 'Disablement Organizations' or something similar. The telephone directory is not the only place to look. Many other directories will be available in your local public library. Once located, an organization with a good information system – and for the necessary depth of information this will probably be held on computer index – should be able to provide you with all the necessary contacts. It cannot be stated too strongly that precious energy can be wasted if one seeks to locate by oneself every organization that may be able to offer help. Remember, the personnel who set up and run these services do so because they want the service to be used. If they are under-used, there is a danger they will have to close. They are only too happy to assist.

There should be a Citizens' Advice Bureau and there may also be a Council of Community Services or Council of Voluntary Services which act as co-ordinators for organizations in the voluntary sector. There may also be a Volunteer Bureau which can match someone's needs with willing volunteers. There will probably be Carers' Groups which are also run on a voluntary basis in or near your locality.

## The Clergy

A clergyman can have an important function, visiting and listening. At such a time one's attitude to religion will not be considered important. The laying-on of hands is acknowledged as giving help and peace to the dying, and arrangements can be made for a visit from a spiritual healer. The holding of a small service may also be an uplifting experience for the entire family.

## Chiropody and Hairdressing

Many chiropodists and hairdressers offer a visiting service, and their attentions can do wonders. They are best located via personal recommendation, but a local information service for the disabled ought to be able to suggest (and maybe even recommend) suitable people.

## THE EMOTIONAL SIDE OF CARING AT HOME

Caring for a dying loved one at home should be a decision entered into freely and without unreasonable pressure being applied by others of the opinion that this is the right thing to do. Those undertaking this role will know they are doing the right thing. They may consider it a duty; they may consider it a return for the love that has been shown to them, or there may be other reasons. The essential aspect, though, is wanting to care for that dying loved one. Such devotion will not be without its difficulties. There may be good back-up help from one or more of the aforementioned organizations, but there will still be emotions to face up to.

## Feeling Left Out

Others may convince themselves that casual socializing is not a proper activity for someone looking after a dying loved one:

'Of course, Sally has such a burden to face; naturally, she wouldn't want to come to our cocktail evening. We'll ask her when her situation is different.' Sally, a forty-seven year old single woman looking after her dying mother, was simply aching to be invited out. She had been caring for her mother for six months and she intended to go on looking after her until the end. But how she longed to have a break and join in ordinary everyday activities, just occasionally. She would have liked to arrange a social evening at home but felt precluded because she was convinced that either nobody would turn up or that those who did would be embarrassed by her situation. She felt she was being left out of invitations because people were afraid of saying the wrong thing, or perhaps of being reminded of a situation which they might have to face one day; or maybe they felt her presence would cast a gloom over the proceedings. No one seemed to realize that she longed to talk about anything that would take her mind off the daily routine for just a couple of hours.

Good intentions on the part of others can sometimes have the opposite effect. It would have been better if Sally had been invited and allowed to decide for herself whether to accept. A break might have enabled her to recharge the batteries, giving her added strength in her caring role.

## Anger and Sadness

Anger and sadness may alternate during the course of caring for a dying loved one: outrage at the unfairness of fate, at the injustice of them being denied fulfilment of their potential, or at the emotional and physical pain they are forced to go through; sadness at the prospect of never being able to talk with them and not to hold them again.

## Feelings of Loss

Sometimes it may be felt that those being cared for have, in a way, already been lost. The effects of illness may have changed

47

their personality; they may no longer be present in temperament. The carer has to mourn the loss of the person they once knew in addition to facing the prospect of mourning his or her physical demise. This burden can make the emotional task of caring much more difficult.

## Role Change

It can be upsetting to have to take on the role of caregiver to a parent who may no longer be able to cope. We have certain expectations of life; for example, that children outlive parents, and that parents look after children. Those taking on the role, though, may consider that they are, in a way, repaying their parent for a lifetime of love, and thus any difficulties encountered are far outweighed by their debt of gratitude.

A similar situation may arise in looking after a very dependent husband or wife. The relationship changes dramatically, the usual marital roles being exchanged for that of parent and dependant.

## The Unwelcome Visitor

This category includes not only those whom one would rather not see, but also those who simply don't know when to leave. Such people can become a nuisance, adding to the burden of both the dying one and the carer. It is best to tell such people from the start that visiting is strictly limited, and if it is simply not the best of days for visiting, never be afraid to put them off. This applies especially to visitors who turn up without warning. Their convenience and welfare are unimportant (apart from the usual courtesies). The well-being of the dying and their carers must take priority.

## THE HOSPICE MOVEMENT

Entering a hospice may become necessary for one of three reasons:

1   A short stay to bring the pain and symptoms under control.

2   To provide a respite for the carers.

3   Because the patient's condition has changed and/or because the facilities at home have become inappropriate.

The word hospice has its origins in the Latin word *hospitium* which means hospitality, inn or lodging. In medieval times the word referred to a resting place for weary travellers; over the centuries the word has gradually come to encompass establishments housing the sick.

The modern movement began during the latter part of the 1960s when St Christopher's Hospice began caring for patients with far advanced malignant diseases. It was founded by Dame Cicely Saunders, who began her career as a nurse, became a lady almoner, and later qualified as a physician. She became a Dame of the British Empire in 1982, and in 1990 a Companion of Honour. The role played by Dame Cicely and St Christopher's in researching and promoting understanding of the problems of the terminally ill is recognized the world over.

The main objectives of the hospice movement are to enable patients to achieve a real quality of life in the time remaining to them, and to provide support to their families. Hospice workers are also prepared to give bereavement care and support for as long as is necessary.

Controlling physical pain is only one of the tasks a hospice team undertakes. Helping to alleviate the emotional pain of someone who is dying is possibly an even more important function. Concern for the loved ones who will be left behind; fear of dying itself; the distress caused by ambitions unfulfilled; these are all aspects which the hospice team understands and helps with, in confidence and with honesty. It is important for the well-being of the dying, too, that the ones who are to remain behind should be emotionally prepared for what is going to happen, and given full support. Hospice workers consider the family of a dying loved one to be a major part of the care team, and their supportive role with the relatives does not end with the death of the loved one.

An important aspect of hospice care is its informal atmosphere. There are no visiting hours. Personal possessions are encouraged, and it is not uncommon for a patient's favourite item of furniture to move temporarily to the hospice as well. Familiar and favourite things are encouraged as being good both for hospice residents and for their nearest and dearest.

The emotional needs of patients and their carers can sometimes be overlooked by hospitals, although recently some have taken the positive step of engaging qualified nursing counsellors to give advice and support to the dying and their loved ones. Longer-term bereavement help may also be offered. Their contribution may be especially valuable if it is not possible to let a dying person know the kind of time span that is remaining, and where he or she may be spending a disproportionate amount of it in hospital – for example, in cases of terminal cardiac illnesses.

## Hospital Support Teams

The Hospice Movement has introduced the hospice approach into acute hospitals. There are more than forty hospital-based Support Teams in the UK. The first was established in St Thomas' Hospital, London in 1977.

## Home Care Services

These have already been covered but it is appropriate to add that most Home Care Teams are funded by Cancer Relief Macmillan Fund and take the name 'Macmillan Nursing Service'. Referral is through a GP or a district nurse. A similar service is also provided through Marie Curie Cancer Care. This will involve day and night care, where necessary. There is a high demand for night nursing, mainly to give relatives a much needed break. It is administered at local level by the National Health Service. At present, there are about 277 Home Care Teams in the UK and Eire; 102 of them are attached to hospice in-patient units.

## Macmillan Continuing Care Units

There are twelve continuing Care Units, each consisting of between ten and twenty-five beds. These were initially funded by Cancer Relief Macmillan Fund and built in the grounds of NHS hospitals. They are now run by the NHS. Additions have now been made by Macmillan, wholly or in part, and are run as independent hospices.

## The Sue Ryder Foundation

The Sue Ryder Foundation Homes care for patients with a wide range of terminal illnesses. Referral is usually through a GP.

## Marie Curie Cancer Care

Marie Curie Cancer Care provides homes and nearly 5,000 Marie Curie nurses for nursing patients in their own homes. Referrals for the homes are usually through a GP or hospital consultant. The home nursing service can be requested locally through the District Nursing Service Officer responsible for Community Nursing Services.

## Financial Considerations

Generally there is no charge for admission to a hospice. However, for the small number where there is no statutory funding a contribution may be requested.

# THE FEELINGS OF THOSE WHO ARE DYING

It may be as difficult for the dying to talk openly about their feelings, anxieties and fears as it is for their loved ones. Whilst some relationships allow honest and open discussion of feelings as a normal part of everyday conversation, others do not, and here the dying will be left to grieve inwardly for themselves and for their loved ones.

The dying have anxieties and fears which those with a reasonable expectation of life can try to understand. Their greatest fears are probably those of suffering and of losing control over their lives. They may fear decision-making being taken out of their hands; they may dread becoming a burden because of their dependence on others. They may fear losing their identity, no longer having freedom of choice about what they do. Financial worries, and concern for the care of their remaining loved ones, may be a source of acute anxiety.

## Preparation

The knowledge that one is dying brings with it a form of preparation that is unique to each person. There may be a need to examine one's life and evaluate one's achievements. The past may even be viewed in a romantic way, providing much comfort. There may be a deep concern with religion, and the meaning and purpose of life. This may be all too easily dismissed by the insensitive and callous as a morbid obsession or a sign of senility. This is not the case, however; it is a sign of a need for preparation which must be accorded the respect it deserves. This can also be a time for making up quarrels, for reconciliation, for making amends, and for putting life's difficulties into perspective.

The future may also be considered by the dying. In some respects they might be said to have certain advantages over those who do not know the likely time span allotted to them. They can review their wills, decide whether property should be sold or bequeathed intact; make arrangements for beloved pets to be looked after; in short, the dying can exercise considerable power and influence as benefactors.

They may wish to be commemorated in a way which reaches beyond the confines of the family; for example, there is the park bench donated in the name of a local person, or the university wing named after its benefactor. This can be a way of satisfying a natural desire to leave one's mark on the world. It may be felt there will always be someone curious as to the identity of the person behind the name.

## Stages

Studies of how the dying respond to their situation were developed in the 1960s. The notable American pioneering psychiatrist in the field, Dr Elizabeth Kubler-Ross, was of the opinion that there were stages of emotions, but that the intensity of each stage varied with the person concerned. The stages consisted of denial, anger, bargaining, depression and acceptance. Subsequent studies have tended to disagree with a definable stage theory, and are inclined towards the idea that while such stages do exist, some may be absent and their order cannot be predicted.

**Denial** No one denies that we are all mortal – it is just that now is not the time for our mortality to be proved. There may be a need to cling to hope; for example, the hope that a miracle cure will suddenly be found. Some may continue to deny and keep hope alive for a very long time. Others – perhaps those who have greeted the news with a degree of relief at the prospect of an end to their suffering – may make little or no denial. Again, denial may alternate with periods of belief, gradually leading to acceptance.

**Anger** The need to vent anger may be totally absent in some, yet very necessary for others. It is most likely in the young, the dynamic or those who feel that they are being cheated out of fulfilling their ambitions. It is least likely in the very elderly and the severely disabled. The most likely target for anger is God. Extreme anger may be unpleasant for others and coping with it may be difficult, but it can lead to a greater understanding of a dying loved one and of the anguish he or she is suffering. It should not be suppressed for the benefit of clinical convenience, and if necessary, specialized help should be sought to help a dying person through this violent emotion.

**Bargaining** There may be a wish to try in some way to delay what is now accepted as inevitable, by bargaining. Such attempted bargains will usually be struck with God, perhaps through a priest or clergyman. The dying may need to fulfil just one last act, or perhaps the bargain is that the end be delayed indefinitely, or that the pain be lessened in exchange for a promise or series of promises to God. This kind of bargaining is evident throughout history: there have always been such attempts to win God's mercy, for example, by commissioning a church, or helping the poor, in exchange for a little more time in this world. Dr Kubler-Ross is of the opinion, however, that despite a promise not to ask for more, once the postponement is granted the promise is rarely, if ever, kept.

**Depression** This arises as a result of the confirmation of one's worst fears. It is accepted that there is no longer any point in trying to deny or delay or in becoming angry; this is a period of mourning, the period of grieving for one's own life. For those who have led a good life in the religious sense, this may be a time when all that was previously valued becomes suddenly meaningless. They may even deny God's existence, or believe that He has betrayed them, leaving them alone, afraid and isolated. Depression also stems from the realization that those things that are held dear will soon be lost.

Depression may be deepened if those closest to the dying refuse to admit that there is now no hope of recovery, thereby creating a situation where the dying are left to grieve, to the end, by themselves.

**Acceptance** This is the most peaceful time for a dying loved one. It is the time when preparation is complete, and there is a readiness, perhaps even a willingness, to receive death. It would be wrong to say that all fear has now been overcome and that all anger and all depression have now disappeared; these emotions may still exist, but in a much milder form.

## THE NEEDS OF THOSE WHO ARE DYING

The dying, *because* they are dying, can easily be misunderstood by those around them who may consider them now to be different. It is possible, also, that some people feel a degree of fear of the dying, and consequently may put up barriers to protect themselves. They may have an unconscious need to reject that which provokes fear, and to pretend that pain does not exist. A dying person, though, has wants and needs just like anyone else; their situation renders these wants and needs more specific, and involves the co-operation of others in order for them to be satisfied.

The lives of the dying have now been circumscribed by a time span; they wish, quite naturally, to use that precious time well and to make the remainder of their lives as meaningful as possible. Their wants and needs should be respected; minor rules and regulations ought not to be a bar to the achievement of their goals.

The dying should not have to die alone. This is meant not only in the sense of the physical presence of others, but also in the sense of the presence of those to whom it is possible to relate. Such people will not be obtrusive; they will allow the dying person the freedom to express their own thoughts, feelings, and emotions, and will be sympathetic to different moods; they will know when their presence is no longer required and also when it is needed again. They will not seek to deceive and will answer questions with honesty. People spend their lives communicating; it would be a tragedy for life to end without communication. There may be areas of pain or unspoken emotions on either side which *need* to be expressed, thereby completing the communication process within the relationship.

The dying have the right to be looked after by people who are prepared to allow them to participate in care decisions.

The dying have the right to die with peace and dignity.

# FINANCIAL BENEFITS

## Attendance Allowance

This is a tax-tree allowance for adults and children, aged six months or over, who are severely disabled either physically or mentally and who need a lot of looking after. There is no upper age limit. It is not means tested and there are no contribution conditions. To qualify, one of the following conditions must be met:

**1**                       **During the Day**
  (i) Frequent attention throughout the day in connection with bodily functions; OR
  (ii) Continual supervision throughout the day in order to avoid substantial danger to oneself or to others

**2**                       **Or, at Night**
  (i) Prolonged or repeated attention is required from another person in connection with bodily functions; OR
  (ii) In order to avoid substantial danger to oneself or others, 'another person to be awake for a prolonged period or at frequent intervals for the purpose of watching over you' is required.

If one of the conditions is met, the applicant will qualify for the lower rate. If one of the day conditions *and* one of the night conditions is met, the applicant will qualify for the higher rate. It is paid to the person actually needing the help. It is not taxable.

The 1990 Social Security Act has abolished the old rule of a six-month qualifying period before the higher rate of Attendance Allowance can be paid, in cases of terminal illness.

This was a particularly inequitable rule for those with less than six months to live. The new Social Security Act, 1990, interprets terminal illness as being 'at any time if at that time [you suffer] from a progressive disease and [your] death in consequence of that disease can reasonably be expected within six months'. This will greatly assist someone with a terminal illness to remain at home.

In this situation it is important to discuss the claim with a GP, to enable it to be made quickly. Once submitted, *a notice of an award* should be received within ten to fourteen days.

It is also important to remember that should a claim be turned down, a *review* of the decision can be asked for. Alternatively, should circumstances change, a fresh application can be made.

A dying loved one does not have to claim personally. This can be done by any competent person in the claimant's name and will most likely be made by those closest. If this is not possible, GPs can submit a claim on their patients' behalf, which would obviously save much anxiety and distress.

## Invalid Care Allowance

Invalid Care Allowance is a benefit for people of working age who spend at least thirty-five hours a week caring for a severely disabled person. It is not means-tested and does not depend on contributions. It is a taxable benefit and is counted with other benefits for the purposes of income if Social Security income benefits are claimed. The person being looked after must be in receipt of Attendance Allowance at either of the two rates. The allowance is not payable if more than a limited amount (less expenses) is earned by the claimant.

## Mobility Allowance

Mobility Allowance is a non means-tested benefit which is designed to help those who are unable or virtually unable to walk, or where the exertion required to walk would, in itself, constitute a danger to the claimant's life, or would be likely to lead to a serious deterioration in health. The benefit cannot be claimed by someone after their sixty-sixth birthday. It is a non-taxable benefit.

Besides these benefits, those with low incomes will be entitled to other benefits under the Income Support system. There may also be help with such things as prescriptions, eyesight tests and dental care.

Organizations such as Citizens' Advice Bureaux or DIAL (Disablement Information and Advice Line) will explain what entitlements are available and assist in making claims. Remember, these benefits are a citizen's right, not a charity offered by a state-run philanthropic society.

## Grants

Grants may be available from organizations such as The National Society for Cancer Relief or the Marie Curie Foundation, for essentials such as night nursing. Look into the possibility of obtaining a grant from the Independent Living Fund. An application form is obtainable from PO Box 183, Nottingham NG8 3RD. It should be noted, however, that this is an income-related benefit.

## Proposed Changes from 1992

At the time of writing, the Government proposes the introduction of a new benefit, the Disability Living Allowance, from April 1992, for new claimants whose disability begins before the age of sixty-five. It will extend help to less severely disabled people and will also incorporate under the same umbrella the help currently provided through the Attendance Allowance and the Mobility Living Allowance schemes. Once awarded, the Disability Living Allowance will continue to be paid irrespective of age, provided the criteria for qualification continue to be met. Attendance Allowance will remain to provide help for people whose disability begins after the age of sixty-five.

The Disability Allowance will have two separate components, a care component, paid at three different levels, and a mobility component, paid at two levels. People will be able to qualify for either or both components, with the rates and assessment criteria for the upper level of the mobility component and the upper two levels of the care component continuing along similar lines to those currently employed for Mobility and Attendance Allowance.

The initial rate of the care component will be awarded to people who need help with self-care during the day but less frequently than those who currently qualify for Attendance Allowance. People who have care needs only at the beginning and end of the day, for example, but who are otherwise able to take care of themselves, will, for the first time, be able to receive help.

The initial rate of the mobility component will be awarded to people who are not independently mobile and who do not otherwise fulfil the current criteria for Mobility Allowance.

Like Mobility Allowance, the Disability Allowance will be awarded only in respect of disability occurring before the age of sixty-five. There will be no upper age limit for continued payment of either the care or mobility component, provided the criteria continue to be met. At the time of writing there is an upper age limit of eighty for payment of Mobility Allowance. Well before then, when the Disability Allowance is introduced, the Government intends to remove the upper age limit for payment of Mobility Allowance to those already receiving it.

At present, there is an important difference in the conditions for Attendance Allowance and Mobility Allowance, as already mentioned. There is a six-month qualifying condition for Attendance Allowance, except for those who are terminally ill. There is no qualifying period for Mobility Allowance at the time of writing. For people who will be entitled to both the care and mobility components, it is proposed to introduce a common qualifying period of three months to eliminate the necessity for two separate medical assessments.

The Disability Allowance will require a single claim and a single medical examination for either or both of the mobility and care components. Emphasis will also be placed on

59

written evidence from GPs, social workers and voluntary organizations, placing, it is hoped, less emphasis on medical examinations which are known to beget injustices.

There will be a new adjudication and appeals structure for the new benefit to replace the existing arrangements, and it is anticipated that the new appeal tribunals will include someone with experience of disabled people's needs instead of being composed largely of medical experts.

# 5 Bereavement and Disability

Caring for a loved one may be an act which continues over many years. The initial relationship will not necessarily be one where bereavement is foreseeable. Many disabled people's life expectations are similar to those without a disability. (Indeed, the term 'disability' can be somewhat misplaced when arbitrarily applied to someone who has lost the ability to walk, for example. The substitute method of propulsion can, in many ways, negate the term, and the disability is only in the eyes of the beholder for whom the absence of this particular faculty in another human being remains a problem.) Consequently, either partner can become the bereaved. The partners may be of the same or a different generation.

What will be the impact on the remaining loved one? Will those in the caring role consider themselves free of a burden, or will there be an emptiness at suddenly being deprived of a way of life which may have gone on for many years? How will the bereaved handicapped person cope now that their devoted caregiver is no longer there? These two aspects will be considered, firstly, from the perspective of the person providing the care; secondly, from that of the person in receipt of the care.

## CARING

About one-fiftieth of the population is caring at home for someone who is disabled, ill or elderly. The term 'carer' is not entirely satisfactory and some people may even find it disagreeable, but it is now generally accepted as a less than perfect description of a particular role. The Oxford English Dictionary now records it, unrecognized though it was as late

61

as the 1986 edition. The task of caring often falls upon the shoulders of the nearest female relative, as a duty expected of them. Society is quite happy to let them perform this important caring role and will not demand any special qualifications – in contrast to the relatively high academic qualifications often needed for the most trivial of paid employment. Of course, if special qualificatons *were* demanded then the entire machinery of our 'caring society' would simply grind to a halt. Therefore, pragmatism is substituted for idealism in a situation which would not be tolerated in any business. Politicians of every persuasion acknowledge the vital role and the skills of carers in society, but only rarely carry forward their praise and gratitude into meaningful fiscal legislation.

There are many categories of people receiving care: those with disorders which necessitate lifelong support and attention; those suffering from disease or accidental injury; those who are infirm, frail or confused because of age. In every case the carer will be called upon to perform tiring and demanding tasks involving time and patience. A whole range of skills will be necessary, as the carer takes on the role of nurse, care attendant and companion, and these activities may well extend to the hours of night as well. They will be over and above the normal household duties. Family life, social life and even a paid working life may have to be fitted in, too, with limitations and restrictions inevitably taking their toll.

The amount of time spent caring varies, of course, according to circumstances. Nearly fifty per cent of carers spend between one and four years caring with about half as many spending between five and nine years, and a quarter caring for up to one year.

## A Changed Lifestyle

The task of caring for a loved one is demanding and exhausting both mentally and physically, especially in the case of carers who are themselves of advancing years. The everyday problems of normal life can seem insignificant in comparison with those encountered by someone who has embraced the responsibility of caring. Living with difficulties becomes a way of life. Opportunities become limited, if not non-existent; this can be especially hard where they might have led to an increased income and an improved standard of living, and seems particularly unfair since caring often imposes an additional financial strain, and extra income is needed just to maintain the status quo.

## The Family

The task of caring may involve a dual role, even a triple role for some. There may be family responsibilities, and possibly responsibilities associated with being employed, as well as to the person needing care. With such pressures, the stresses and strains on a family can be immense. Some family members may feel neglected with so much time being taken up by the caring role. Carers may feel a loss of identity and privacy, being 'on call' all the time, and unable to do anything outside the caring role without first making elaborate preparations, and arrangements, and then having to keep one eye on the clock.

On the other hand, the situation may lead to a greater bond between the loved one, the carer and the rest of the family. Petty bickering and thoughtlessness may disappear altogether, and each individual's true potential may be realized in such a situation.

## Finance

The care of a very ill or severely handicapped person imposes costs without regard for ability to pay, and the effects of such an additional financial burden can be considerable. Special equipment can be astronomically expensive and carers may be unable to afford essential items. It is tragic that most of those suffering from congenital deformities or crippling diseases have no financial recompense; our legal system does not recognize a 'no fault' system of compensatory payments. Consequently, unless negligence can be proved, desperately needed resources are not forthcoming. Those who do meet with success through the courts have often spent years battling to gain relatively modest payments, which are reduced further because of the legal costs. It is only the few awards which do eventually meet with considerable success that attract news headlines; the majority do not. Statutory allowances are seen as being limited by what a civilized society can reasonably afford. All political parties in opposition denounce the government in power for its uncaring attitude to the sick and disabled, but the situation continues when the roles are reversed.

The cost of extra quantities of everyday items alone can be considerable; the winter months can mean considerably higher fuel bills. There is no discount for purchasing electricity or gas in bulk. Normal *business* transactions allow buyers of large quantities of most products a discount. Not so for domestic consumers of essential energy supplies, though sympathetic consideration will, of course, be given to those who find difficulty in paying. Customer liaison officers should always be approached in this case, and organizations such as Citizens' Advice Bureaux will be able to advise and make approaches to utility companies on someone's behalf.

Wear and tear on fixtures and fittings can necessitate frequent replacement. Appliances which are not really designed for use in a conventionally furnished home can impose immense strains on the décor. Those who are receiving Income Support may obtain priority help from the Social Fund and receive financial help towards replacement, but this will, of course, be administered within a tight overall budget so the help is likely to be limited.

## Employment

Many of working age may have to give up or modify their working lives. The usual working week is tailored to meet the needs of a male-oriented society. The majority of carers are women, who become carers at a much earlier age than men, most male caregivers being at or nearing retirement age, when such matters as pension rights have been secured. As a result, men are deterred from taking on a caring role by the rigid expectations of employers, but even when the female carer is the major breadwinner, she still has to adapt to a male-structured environment. The consequent restrictions on her working life can mean loss of promotion or training opportunities, and a reduction in or limit to the kind of salary that can be achieved. She may even have to seek lower-paid employment just because of the conveniences of hours and location. The need to carry on working may not necessarily be financial: employment may be fulfilling in itself; it can also provide a necessary change of environment and relief from the pressures of caring.

Normal domestic crises are usually given sympathetic consideration but the continuing crisis of caring rarely meets with a similar response from employers, unfortunately. By adapting to an employee's vital needs by, for example, offering flexible working hours and extended leave, they could do much to relieve pressures and help her or him to be a more efficient worker. Sadly, though, employees in this situation are often seen as having a reduced commitment to work in comparison with colleagues who are not so encumbered.

## The Physical and Emotional Welfare of Carers

Caring, by its very nature, is physically oriented. There will be lifting tasks to perform, and some will be very heavy. In hospital these would probably be carried out by several nursing staff – and quite rightly. Home caregivers, though, often have to perform feats of quite unusual strength, irrespective of age or state of health, and consequently they are vulnerable to such physical problems as bad backs or painful legs that would place many employees on the sick list with perhaps a referral to the Health and Safety Executive!

The role of carer can be stressful, naturally, depending on the relationship between the persons concerned. Studies have shown that the closer the personal relationship the easier it is to cope with stress, although dealing with the intimate tasks may be more difficult. Stress, therefore, can be minimal or it can be at a level that induces such symptoms as feeling run down, high blood pressure, headaches, insomnia and even skin complaints. It can be increased by additional worries over finance and family pressures.

When someone agrees to take on the main responsibility for caring, it often transmutes into that person having the *absolute* responsibility. This can cause emotional distress. Feelings of anger at being isolated, and at the assumption by others that providing assistance with bodily functions is his or her sole responsibility. Grief for the impending loss of the loved one, and the effort of taking into account the needs of other members of the family, can all combine to create stressful symptoms.

## Socializing

The demands of caring often impose a restricted social life. Energy levels can be low, time is often limited; friendships, too, tend to lapse as a result of the demands of the caring role. Sometimes the carer has no social life whatsoever.

It may, of course, be possible to take the loved one for outings or visits, although inevitably these will be limited because of such restrictions as lack of wheelchair access and so on. There are, however, an increasing number of specialized publications listing places that can accommodate wheelchairs, and many booksellers now have sections devoted to aspects of disablement.

Overcoming access problems may sometimes be only the initial hurdle. It may be felt that some places are out of bounds because of other people's reactions to a wheelchair user. Visiting friends can present problems because of the difficulties of mobility and access, and besides, continually bringing along one's dependent loved one may put the friendship under strain. The visit, too, is likely to be fairly short and possibly unsatisfactory, anyway. Some people may be nervous at the prospect of a visit by someone whose charge perhaps needs personal and constant attention.

If one's present friends and acquaintances appear reluctant to adapt themselves to such a major change in one's circumstances, it may be necessary to seek new contacts. These days there are numerous self-help groups which may be founded locally, or which may be branches of national associations. Their functions range from giving information to providing opportunities for socializing.

There is a wide diversity both in the type and membership of carers' groups. They may be professionaly based or they may have been started at grass roots level because nothing of the kind existed. Some groups engage in active lobbying whilst others concentrate on the day-to-day needs of the carer, and provide a forum for the exchange of information and help. They offer excellent opportunities to make new friendships.

## Holidays

Taking a holiday has been a very real problem for the carer: the loved one cannot be left, and it is equally impossible to take him or her on holiday with all the attendant problems of accommodation, access, suitable care in an unsuitable setting, as well as having to cope with the reactions of other holidaymakers.

However, in recent years the needs of such people have increasingly been met, with all the arrangements being taken care of by the holiday organizers. The whole family can take a holiday together, and if one's financial circumstances are difficult, there are organizations prepared to meet the total cost, if necessary.

Organizations such as the Across Trust will provide all the care facilities that are needed – en route as well as at the destination – and there will be many able helpers, too, to provide accompaniment. The Holiday Care Service matches needs to what is available, making further searching for something suitable unnecessary. (See page 207 for useful addresses.)

## Respite Care

The concept of respite care is fairly new, a recent acknowledgement of the needs of those who are caring. It is recognized that for the welfare of all concerned, the carer must have the occasional opportunity to take a break. Where there has been a diagnosis of cancer, there is often good respite care support and this has been covered in the previous chapter. Other distressing terminal illnesses, especially those that are comparatively rare, may not have the same ready availability of respite care; however, there is an increasing awareness of the need for this facility, and it is to be hoped that more support in this area will become available.

Where respite care in an optimum environment cannot be found, alternatives will have to be considered. Nursing or residential homes may have short-term placement facilities. Alternatively, the local authority may agree to provide help; failing this, a private establishment will have to be sought, and help towards the cost may be available. A short-term stay in hospital will perhaps be the only alternative, although if care only is required and not treatment, it is not, of course, the ideal environment. The necessary personal attention may not be available where such care facilities are rare, but some hospitals have introduced such a scheme, setting aside a special part of the hospital for such use.

Regular respite care during each week may be more desirable than two or three weeks' absence from the loved one. A hospital may provide day care facilities for those who need regular treatment or specialized care. It can also arrange such personal services as hairdressing, nail cutting, etc. Special transport will invariably be provided.

Of course, having made the best arrangements in the world, the carer may meet with reluctance or even outright refusal on the part of the loved one to be moved. The problem will either have to be overcome by persuasion or the dependant will simply have to be capitulated to; the latter might be particularly necessary where the loved one is elderly.

## A Suitable Environment in which to Care

Physical devotion is only half the answer in the struggle to achieve a reasonable standard of care. The proper tools will ensure a far more successful result, but too often the carer is unaware of their existence, and consequently, 'making do' can be the norm. For instance, probably the two most difficult physical tasks of caring are helping one's charge up the stairs, and bathing. Caregivers can still be found today physically hauling their charges up and down the stairs, sometimes on their backs. Stair rails and ramps, however, can be provided as part of the local social services entitlement. An even better solution is the installation of a stair lift, which can be provided by the local social services in certain circumstances. Very often, the benevolent fund of a former employing organization would be only too willing to help, especially so in the case of ex-servicemen. The relevant welfare officer should be approached. Groups of local businessmen such as the Lions are often benefactors. Second-hand stairlifts in perfectly good condition can sometimes be bought for a fraction of their new price. Sometimes generous bereaved people will give away such items of equipment where they are desperately needed. However, a professional inspection of any second-hand item is recommended.

Where bathing is concerned, minimal adaptations may be required such as the provision of a suitable bath seat and a handrail. These items should be provided almost automatically by the local social services, with a minimum of delay. More specialized equipment, such as a bath hoist, is again available from the local social services in essential situations.

Reluctance on the part of caregivers to seek an improvement in their situation is a major reason for the lack of mechanical aids in the home. Older caregivers may believe that requesting help is asking for charity, or, perhaps that it might be interpreted by the loved one as evidence that he or she has become a burden. Perhaps there is also the feeling that social services provisions are just not worth the bother, or a fear, often quite without foundation, that a means test must be taken before help can be offered.

At the same time, blame must be attached to the authorities for not publicizing sufficiently what help is available. Targeting those most obviously in need of help, through GPs, for example, needs to be pursued more vigorously. Many people just do not know where to start looking for information. It is often the case that knowledge of the help available is discovered quite by chance, and unless very good cause can be shown for not having applied earlier, backdating, for example, social security benefits can be extremely difficult. Caregivers are often completely baffled by the fact that there are apparently readily available resources for institutional care, but only a fraction of the help seems to be available for caring at home.

Caring for a loved one at home may mean that space becomes restricted. If it becomes impossible to climb the stairs, a room on the ground floor may have to be adapted. Where space is already at a premium, other family members may have to share bedrooms, with the corresponding reduction in privacy. Even when adapted or purpose-built housing is available, there may be a lack of space for the other members of the family. It may also entail having to move to a new area, thereby losing contact with old friends and acquaintances. Fortunately, such needs are increasingly being recognized, with housing associations providing much more purpose-built accommodation.

## The Legal Management of a Loved One's Affairs

It may well be the case that looking after personal and financial matters is beyond the capability of a dependant. Everyday matters such as collecting pensions or benefits should pose no problem. The Department of Social Security, for example, will provide a form for the carer to sign in such an eventuality. When more complicated matters arise such as essential financial transactions or matters relating to a business or the sale of the home, legal advice should be sought as soon as possible. There are two ways of taking over a person's affairs: by Power of Attorney, and the Court of Protection.

**Power of Attorney** One can only be granted a Power of Attorney by the consent of a mentally capable person. There are two types of Power: Ordinary and Enduring.

70

An Ordinary Power will automatically lapse if the person granting it later becomes mentally incapable. Recent legislation has modified the old rule whereby a Power always ceased upon the mental incapability of the person granting it. The Enduring Power of Attorney Act, 1985, permits the validation to continue provided legal consent was possible in creating the original Power, i.e. that a continuation in the event of a mental incapacity was made clear at the time *and* there was compliance with the legal formalities. Alternatively, an Enduring Power can take effect only if and when the person granting it becomes unable to deal with his or her own affairs.

For an Enduring Power of Attorney to take effect it must be registered with the Court of Protection. The Court will only give consent to register if it is satisfied with the evidence of the donor's mental incapacity and if all the procedures regarding notices etc., have been followed. The Power is administered by the Court of Protection.

Ending a Power can be achieved in several ways. If a Power is granted for a specific period, or for a particular purpose, it will automatically lapse when that time expires or the purpose has been achieved. A Power also ends automatically if the donor or attorney dies, or the attorney becomes bankrupt. A Power, whether it is ordinary or enduring, can be withdrawn by the donor as long as he or she is mentally capable. However, if the Power has been revoked and the attorney continues to act on the donor's behalf, being legally bound by certain transactions could still be possible.

In Scotland, granting a Power to someone for the purpose of acting on another's behalf is technically known as a Factory of Commission and while the rules are different, it is often referred to as a Power of Attorney. There is no equivalent of an Enduring Power under Scottish law, however.

**The Court of Protection**  When a person is deemed mentally incapable, a Receiver can be appointed by the Court of Protection, such as a solicitor or a member of the family, to conduct the affairs of that person. The Receiver is closely

71

supervised by the Court and a fee is charged for this purpose. It is based on the income of the person on whose behalf the conduct of affairs is taking place.

There is also a Short Order Procedure of the Court of Protection, where no fee is charged. It enables essential financial obligations to be met where such obligations are not being fulfilled, e.g. because of occasional confusion over whether bills have been paid or not. The address of the Court of Protection is: Stewart House, 24 Kingsway, London WC2B 6HD (Telephone: 071 405 4300).

It is also possible to make someone the subject of Guardianship proceedings. The powers conferred here are firstly, to require the person to reside at a specified place; secondly, to attend at any given time for treatment; and thirdly, to require that access is given to certain named individuals, such as a doctor or welfare worker.

In Scotland, the equivalent of the Court of Protection is the Curator Bonis. In Northern Ireland, the Office of Care and Protection has a parallel role to that of the English court.

**Credit Unions**   These have been a feature of the north of England for some time but are relatively rare in the south. They are a means of borrowing money at very reasonable rates of interest, usually well below the prevailing market rates. They can be formed by any group of people with a similar interest, and are regulated by the Registrar of Friendly Societies. Money can be borrowed at a fixed rate of interest. Savers with a credit union are paid interest gross of tax. The common bond which is necessary for the formation of a credit union is usually defined as one created by people living within a clearly defined area. It may well be that those who are looking after severely disabled loved ones could form such a credit union within a particular area, thereby providing some additional financial help when official assistance will not stretch to certain essential purchases. A credit union operates solely for the benefit of its members, that is, they are the only people who are eligible to borrow. There is no conventional commercial approach to a credit union, its aim usually being to break even after interest payments to savers and administration expenses have been met.

# WHEN THE CARING STOPS

Those who have cared for the disabled have to cope not only with the grief of actual loss, but also with the emptiness that can arise when the routine tasks of everyday caring cease. They may already have experienced different kinds of bereavement whilst caring for their loved one – the loss of a career, curtailed relationships, perhaps a marriage foregone or even broken. Now, in addition to their physical loss, they may find themselves unexpectedly bereaved by the loss of their role as caregiver.

## A Case History: Bob

'My father died about twenty years ago when I was in my late teens, leaving my mother with myself as her only remaining family. She was in her forties and I have to confess that the thought of her remarrying and me ending up with a stepfather was too awful to contemplate. It seems to me now a rather selfish attitude, but then, attitudes towards one's parents are quite funny, really. They're not seen in a sexual light at all. The idea that my mother may have had physical as well as emotional needs would have shocked me. As things turned out she didn't remarry but channelled her energies into new directions. Fortunately, my father had left her fairly well provided for; she became enthusiastically involved in various charitable activities, and was promoted to the Bench as a Justice of the Peace.

'I do not remember much of the time surrounding my father's death. It was obviously a terrible time for my mother. I mostly remember telling myself that I was now part of a one-parent family. This description, until then, had been almost a euphemisn for social deprivation and yet there I was in that very situation ... Upon reflection, my attempts to console my mother as well as trying to come to terms with my own sense of loss seemed grossly inadequate ... My mother recovered from my father's death – at least, I was always led to believe that she had – but now I think that she probably never did fully recover. I am convinced she kept her hurt to herself in order to protect me. She considered my career important, and with hindsight I can only presume that she felt that fully sharing her grief with me would somehow set back my career ambitions. Parents, however, underestimate their children's fortitude.

'My career progressed and my relationship with my mother became very strong over the years. We were extremely good friends; despite a succession of attractive girlfriends I never married – I never fell desperately in love with anyone to the point where getting married was the natural final step. I think it is better to be honest rather than capitulate to social pressures to conform – despite mild worries I may have had from time to time at being labelled as having an Oedipus complex, which is simply not true, or something else, equally untrue!

'My mother first started complaining of headaches towards the end of the summer, about five years ago. She didn't consider them anything to worry about, and it was not until the end of the year that there was the terrible realization that something was seriously wrong, and that she would need looking after for the rest of her life. Combining my career with visits to my mother each day, with associated professional help to hand, did not seem to be an arrangement which would impose too many restrictions, or at least, not at first. I had been warned that her condition was terminal, but no definite answer could be given as to how much time she had remaining.

'A choice soon had to be made between my career and my mother's care needs. Everyone around me made it abundantly, albeit discreetly, clear that I must not let my mother's tragedy become a dominating feature of my life. They finally ventured to tell me, "You have your own life to lead. They can do wonders in nursing homes, these days. They are just like being at home. She will be happy there."

'This was of little consolation to me. To imply that my mother had now become a liability, I found insensitive and tasteless in the extreme. It was not simply a matter for compromise; it was a question of taking responsibility for my mother, my only remaining relative, and deciding, without condescension, what was best for her. Logic dictated that I should arrange a permanent care placing somewhere, and this would unquestionably have met with agreement from my mother as being in *my* best interest. The reality, however, was that it would have signalled the end of my mother's will to carry on. I knew that in this situation her suffering would have been compounded, but that she was prepared to accept it for my sake. I considered that I had no choice other than to return as much care and devotion to her as she had given me during my period of growing up. I did not feel coerced but did hope, profoundly, that I was not taking a decision I would later regret. After all, my life had been relatively successful and I did not know the true meaning of sacrifice and service. Would any deprivation I might later feel alter my attitude towards my mother? Would I start to hold her responsible for dictating the course of my life? Would a real me emerge, forcing me to face the fact that there are limits to my tolerance of those I love? Would I realize that I was not to be the person I had thought I was?

'I have learned that caring for someone else can leave one somewhat isolated. One is certainly regarded as a little odd to want to exchange a life of comparative self-centredness at a so-called prime age, for one of service. It altered my outlook on other people and I realized that some relationships were so shallow as to be worth little or nothing. On the other hand, I learned much about myself. My initial fears about my staying power were, thankfully, without foundation. Helping my mother with her most personal tasks never became a permanent arena of embarrassment. I cannot say why, but I can only assume that I am more able in this respect than I ever gave myself credit for. Together, we found a way of overcoming any such problems. It was always a question of teamwork and never a matter of having to fight difficult odds. We co-operated with each other in a way which led us to becoming even greater friends than before.

'I spent nearly five years caring for my mother and it was only in the last three weeks of her life that specialist hospice care was needed. I have never felt so valued before as a human being. Of course, there were times when I questioned the wisdom of what I was doing. Was it right for a grown man to be incarcerated in a house with his terminally ill mother? What financial rewards would there have been if my career had been allowed to come to fruition? Despite this, my conviction had been reinforced that I *was* doing the right thing. I made many friends who, but for my circumstances, I would never have come into contact with. One of them, Jacquie, has become someone very special in my life. She is a district nurse and her visits were a Heaven-sent opportunity to get to know someone so wonderful.

'I am now officially classified as 'the bereaved relative'. It is funny, I feel almost a different species now. I am approached by so many people offering condolences and I am pleased that so many have come forward to express their feelings of sorrow. I am told that I have done my duty, and that it is now time for me to think of myself, to put myself first for a change. Such statements may make others feel better but it does not do much for me and I am not entirely certain what they mean, in any case. Putting myself first is something I have long since ceased to regard as being necessary or desirable. It may be thought that I have become brainwashed, perhaps even that I have acquired a subservient attitude; but this is nonsense and only serves to demonstrate a complete lack of understanding. I always knew the situation would end sooner or later and I have to admit that there have been times when I hoped it would end sooner. But I now feel bereaved in two ways; firstly, the physical loss of my mother; secondly the loss of my caregiving role, my role as joint team-leader.

'My almost overnight change of lifestyle is very hard to take; it is almost like suddenly losing a limb. I feel I have now lost the freedom to lead my chosen way of life. There were times when I thought how marvellous it would be not to have to follow the rigid daily routine of washing, bathing, dressing and preparing meals for my mother. The situation is now reversed. I miss not having the opportunity to do it. I am, in a way, suffering withdrawal symptoms, and they are going to go on for a long time. Resuming my career will be difficult. In fact, even if I was given the opportunity to return to my old firm tomorrow, I do not think I could face the prospect, for two reasons: firstly, my commercial competitive edge is rusty (in truth, it is more probable I have lost the killer instinct necessary to succeed) secondly, I have to face the fact that I am a changed person and that my future is going to have to complement the last five years, the most important five years of my life.

'I feel very lucky to have been able to get to know my mother so well. The physical tasks in themselves, I do not entirely miss. Ironically, it was the need for physical help that gave us the opportunity to get to know each other so well as equals, and not just as parent and offspring, which I expect would have been the case if her life had been different. Given the choice again, I would willingly return to the day I made my decision five years ago and repeat the experience. I hear people say how they came to terms with losing an elderly parent; but when we start talking it emerges they have had only relatively frequent contact. Of course, I wouldn't seek to devalue their tragedy, but it is difficult for people to realize that losing someone who has literally been your life for five years is something which they cannot hope really to grasp unless they have been through the same experience.

'I have lost a part of myself. I realize I have become institutionalized in a way. I have inherited all of my mother's estate, but I feel as if I have lost my legacy, the legacy of caregiving. It is so difficult to accept that I have so much time to myself: I hear others saying how marvellous it must be to have financial security, that I have "earned" it and "deserve" it. I do not feel as if I have earned anything. I feel only deprivation and heartache.

'It's not easy for a man to express to the world that at the age of forty-five he is grieving so much for his mother: it simply isn't *decent* for a grown man to be so emotional. The only person I feel I can confide in is Jacquie; she is the only one who really seems to understand and, most importantly, seems genuinely to care. There, I even use the word "seems" when it comes to Jacquie; I suppose, at heart, I feel completely alone, possibly even by choice. Some of the blame for this surely has to fall on my shoulders. Perhaps I *want* to feel no one else can truly understand. Perhaps I'm being a little possessive with my mother's memory. . . .

'I had no idea that these five years would propel me into such a different set of values. I know that I am fortunate to have a sound financial base, but I have learned that apart from the necessity of a minimum standard of income, the pursuit of material reward *per se* is neither a desirable or necessary means nor a desirable or necessary end. It is not enough to exist purely for oneself; there are so many people who need so much help, and they are the responsibility of us all. We need to be constantly reminded of suffering in order not to become complacent. . . .

'This philosophizing may seem a long way removed from my own tragic loss, and yet it is so intertwined. Coming to terms with the loss of my mother and my caregiving role will not be easy, but I am hopeful; hopeful that I will heal yet never forget; that I will marry Jacquie and have children, and that they will learn a little of just how special their grandmother was.'

# THE LOSS OF A CAREGIVER

## A Case History: Guy

'Rheumatoid arthritis was diagnosed when I was only seventeen. It took a couple of years really to take effect and when it did Mum and Dad found it very difficult to cope with the situation. They did their best; but it was my sister, Sarah, who took on most of the responsibility for looking after me. I must have been a damned nuisance, whining on about the pain and yelling at her not to be so clumsy when she did her best to help me. I don't know how she put up with me. I must have seemed such an ungrateful little whatsit.

'She and I eventually moved into a ground-floor apartment that had been specially adapted. The Social Services people were really good to us. I don't know why Sarah decided to care for me. We hardly ever talked about it – it just happened, just naturally evolved. But she gave me an independence that I never fully appreciated at the time.

'When Sarah died it seemed as if I'd lost a part of myself. It's such a boring old cliché: songs go on about "Losing you is losing me" or "You're a part of me so don't go". All of these bloody songs seem to be crawling out of the woodwork now. Sometimes I would like to yell at the radio and scream out that they have no idea what they are really talking about. Someone hasn't just walked out on me because of some difficult domestic crisis. My entire world has been devastated – I have lost my best friend – I have also lost, literally, the one person who was able to understand, perfectly, my difficulties. Sarah accepted me for what I was and for what I was able to do. She never looked down on me or treated me as a dependant. I realize now I have been protected from a world full of people who, I am sure, simply regard me now as "That crippled bloke". There was me thinking how wonderful I was, being able to cope, and wondering why other disabled people get so ratty with the common or garden, non-disabled variety. Now I know.

'The thing I really found so hateful after Sarah died was that for the first time in my life I felt I had become classified as some kind of case study, some kind of problem to which a solution had to be found. I had never considered that I might be regarded as a problem before; I had always been protected by Sarah's devotion.

'I feel as if I have been prodded, poked, doubted, believed, laughed at, yet taken seriously. I am not sure any more who I am or what I am. Rheumatoid arthritis is really weird. Some days you can be far better than others. This was just great for Sarah and me because it meant that some days she could snatch a rest. Now I feel I have to put on a bit of an act so as to provide some sort of continuity. I am sure that some people do not believe me when they see my condition fluctuate. I feel I have got to remain in the confounded wheelchair *all* the time, otherwise they assume I am getting better – or worse, that I am simply trying to get their sympathy.

'Pain is so difficult to explain. It must be rather like being deaf. What people do not see they do not sympathize with. I hate making a fuss; but my pain is never confined just to one area; so, when people ask me how the pain is here or how it is there and I tell them that it is somewhere else today, you can almost see their scepticism. I never had to explain this to Sarah. Maybe I should have been allowed to struggle more with the outside world. Maybe I have been too well protected.

'For the first time in my life I now feel like a true dependant. I had no choice other than to come into this home. Nothing was ever said by anyone – all the decisions really were mine. No one offered to take me in and I suppose I did not really expect it of them. But I am sure there was quite a bit of relief when I said it was probably best all round if I came here. I'm no longer part of a team. I'm a patient and I am made to feel like one. People are considerate, of course, but they expect you to conform; they don't want a trouble-maker. It's my individuality that I feel is at stake. I've had to give up the job I had for a few hours each week, as a result of my increased disability. They're now trying to give me occupational therapy to keep my interest going. The bits of housework I was able to manage with Sarah were just terrific. I knew I was genuinely helping her but even if I made a complete cock-up of the whole thing we usually ended up laughing together. Now, everything I do is classified as therapy. Sometimes, I feel like tipping a bowl of soup on the floor and saying, "It's good therapy, you know, getting on your hands and knees to clean it up." I'd like to, but I don't think I'd dare.

'I cannot tell you just how awful it is having to call for help to perform even the simplest of tasks. You have to wait until it is convenient for other people. This came as a terrible blow to me. Sarah always seemed to be there, and even if she wasn't prepared to put me first on every single occasion, it did not matter too much: I was as concerned for her as she was for me. We seemed to have no fixed expectations of each other and that's why we probably worked so well together. Now I realize I'm a person who likes to get things done; but if you are surrounded by people who do not share the same philosophy, frustration sets in and friction can arise. It's nobody's fault, really; it's just a conflict between need and expectation. The

79

thing I dread most is that I shall become so tense inside that I shall burst out at some stage. That will be no good for anyone.

'The word that really weighs heavily on my mind now is "burden". Up until Sarah's death I had felt only incapacitated, never burdensome. What distresses me now are these questions: was Sarah simply hiding her real feelings about me? Did I somehow contribute to her death? Have I been blissfully ignorant that I am responsible for what has happened? Nobody can or will tell me, and I am left with a dreadful feeling of guilt. Did I monopolize her life too much? Would she have survived if it had not been for me?

'The thing I miss most is my sense of partnership. Help is very often given with the best of intentions but it can so easily turn someone into thinking of themselves as being worse than they actually are. I realize it must be difficult for the staff because there's not just me to consider, but if help is given with everything you end up just a cabbage. . . .

'Anyway, here I am and I don't know what the immediate future holds for me now. I visit Mum and Dad and they visit me but that's all it is, just visiting. I receive visits and I make visits, that's all. I feel I'm in a time warp. It would be great to say that, given time, I'm sure I will recover and just have happy memories of my lovely Sarah. But it all seems too unreal.

'I feel I am now going to have to cope with being alone. When others cannot possibly understand, there really doesn't seem to be much alternative. I go through the motions of co-operating when the physical care tasks get going, but I just hope they will end quickly, so as I can get on with being by myself with my thoughts. There's not much point in complaining about the pain. If you've chosen to become a bit of a loner then you're inclined to get less sympathy, anyway. So I keep it to myself as much as possible. It's funny, I can't really withdraw physically from other people so I have to put up with second best, by withdrawing into myself. How I long to be able to share again, though. . . .

'I guess I've a lot of grieving yet to do, before I can get a new life together. As I become used to fending for myself over the coming years, I hope these intense emotions will diminish, gradually, and that *my new life* will come to be *my life*. However, Sarah taught me so much that perhaps, some day, I will try to give to someone else just something of what she was able to give to me. I think I owe it to her.'

# 6 Unexpected Death

The opportunity to prepare for the death of a loved one is not always possible, and the tragedy of losing someone with suddenness may give rise to symptoms of shock and stress that are additional to those already discussed. This chapter will look at two such ways in which a loved one can be lost: by accident, and by the taking of his or her own life.

## BEING TOLD

The breaking of bad news in a compassionate way was discussed in Chapter 2. If this compassionate approach is not made to those who have suffered a sudden loss, there may be little opportunity for them to order their thoughts and elicit information, and they may be left in an agony of not knowing, floundering among a host of unposed questions.

Alternatively, it may be felt kinder to put off revealing the full truth of what has happened in the belief that the delay will offer a degree of cushioning. This strategy usually only serves to confuse the bereaved, and in any case it may have been adopted by those entrusted with breaking the news out of fear of being unable to handle a violent reaction.

Even the most compassionate approach to breaking the news of a loved one's death cannot, of itself, make the task of handling grief more acceptable. It can only begin to form the groundwork for preparing for grief. However, no one should be left in a state of confusion and bewilderment: the bereaved have a right to expect honesty, consideration and support, and time to absorb the news. Nevertheless, if it is not possible to see the deceased loved one – perhaps because of a tragedy far from home – it may well be the case that acceptance of what has happened will be delayed.

# ACCIDENTAL DEATH

The most likely cause of sudden death is accident. A misjudgement, a moment's lack of attention, perhaps having insisted that today was the day for that essential visit instead of tomorrow – each may be seen as the cause of such a tragedy. Accidental death often cannot be accepted for exactly what it is: a tragic accident. There is almost always a desire for blame to be apportioned in some way. The accident cannot be seen as having happened because of a combination of unfortunate circumstances. Someone must have caused such a thing to happen; someone must be guilty, it is felt.

## Blaming Oneself

Being present at the time of the accident often entails feeling a need to shoulder at least part of the blame; some may torment themselves by taking on board all of the blame. There may be an understandable confusion between what they have seen and what they feel they may have done to contribute towards the tragedy. Question upon question will be asked to which there may be no answers. This will only serve to convince that they must be at fault: 'What could I have done to prevent this from happening'? or 'What was my part in all of this'? They may feel also that others are secretly blaming them, and the most innocent of concerned enquiries may be interpreted as the equivalent of an inquisition.

There may also be feelings of having become an outcast, a pariah, of being almost 'unclean' in the Biblical sense.

## A Case History : Lucy

Lucy is in her late twenties and some five years ago the car she was driving collided with her little nephew, who lived opposite her and who suddenly ran out into the road. There was nothing she could have done to avoid him. She had received no warning of his intentions and everyone who witnessed the accident said she was not at fault. However, Lucy could not accept that she was blameless. The car *she* was driving had caused his death. As she saw it, it was a totally black and white situation. Either she had caused his death or she hadn't caused his death. If she hadn't then she was innocent; if she had then she was guilty. There was simply no centre ground. She regarded herself, therefore, as being utterly to blame.

She asked herself constantly whether she needed to arrive home at that precise time. Couldn't she have made it a few minutes earlier or later? She said, 'The feeling that I am responsible for killing someone is just terrible. I have not only deprived that child of his life, I have deprived my sister and brother-in-law of the chance to continue sharing their love with him. I cannot say why I blame myself. I just cannot find any answer to that question. My brother-in-law did blame me terribly at first, but he has made it plain that he no longer feels that way and that he was wrong to have done so. It doesn't seem to make any difference, though. Others have told me to try to put it to the back of my mind now. They don't really understand the anguish I feel. I don't talk about it to anyone any more.

'I feel I have deprived them of so much. I have a daughter who is so full of life that I feel almost guilty at taking her love and affection. I feel I do not have a right to it. I didn't realize at first that these ambivalent feelings of love for my daughter and yet wanting to reject her stemmed from that terrible day. I haven't rejected my daughter's love or my love towards her, though, because I couldn't inflict punishment upon someone who is completely innocent. Yet I still feel guilty at enjoying what my sister and brother-in-law cannot enjoy – because of me. I feel I'm being punished by an unseen force for taking away Stephen's life and I feel that there is nothing I can do to atone. I cannot consider Stephen's part in all this because he is no longer here; there is only me, and the scars run very deep.'

## Reviewing What Has Happened

Although Lucy's sad story is an extreme example, it does show that apportioning blame – finding new reasons to blame – are often inevitable. The details leading up to the tragedy may be reviewed time and time again as the person thinks about what the outcome would have been if events had been just that little bit different. Fact will be mixed with fiction, and the continual reviewing of events and imagined events may even invade dreams. There is a need to try to determine responsibility for the tragedy even if this is not possible. However, it can be a way of trying to incorporate the trauma into one's everyday life, thereby providing the beginnings of an emotional adjustment. Nevertheless, it will seem like an ever-present burden at first, overshadowing one's life to an unbearable extent. One may become abstracted and withdrawn as one's mind obsessively returns again and again to what has happened.

## Complete Loss

An accident may be of such catastrophic proportions that the opportunity to see the mortal remains of a loved one may not be possible. One of the most traumatic experiences is the lack of opportunity to say goodbye with the holding of a funeral service. The knowledge that a loved one has never been found will make it particularly difficult to come to terms with the loss, and to begin the process of what is seen as proper grieving:

'I simply couldn't bear to remove any of his possessions from his room. It just isn't possible if there has been no proper funeral or a Christian service, and we have been denied that opportunity. I always thought that once he returned home I would be able to start getting my house in order and to get on with living again. But it simply hasn't been possible. I'm going to have to make it possible, though. It will be a year to the day soon, and some sort of memorial service is desperately needed.'

## A Memorial Service

A memorial service may be an addition to or a substitute for a traditional funeral service before burial or cremation. In the case of a tragedy where recovering the loved one's body has not been possible, it will be an essential part of the grieving process. There will be a need to share that person with others who also knew and loved him or her. Every memorial service is unique, there is no element of a routine service about it. It is a means of allowing everyone to show their feelings openly and to celebrate the life of the person they have known.

The exceptional thing about a memorial service is that it can be held anywhere if a church or other place of worship is not felt to be appropriate. Perhaps being held at the spot nearest to where the deceased spent their last hours may contribute much to preparing for the path of grief. It can be a comfort to the bereaved to include the loved one's favourite music, poems or prose passages in the service; even to make up their own tribute. Here is one such memorial poem:

## For Michael

No comfort in metaphors
No help to reason
The tides sway at the moon's will,
The leaves must fall their gold to brown,
The fine bright finches slip away,
cicadas thrill for one brief day:
all things have their season ...

Knowing about loss
no way takes loss away.

Yet what is good is
good.
In every living, something's
gained:
Balancing the pitching board, the sail,
lolling in surf and sand,
baby-sleeping, guitaring the melody,
shaping, playing the bounce of the ball, the leap
for the high one, and the delicate
tracery of hands in the pen and the line ....

What was good was
good, and still is
good:
the love for living
and living as love.

Good isn't ever lost:
gold is still the leaf's gift,
Silver under the moon
the remembered, the imagined
crescent wave.

To have known these as good
is to know good in being.

Not loss,
but like the leaf's gold,
the heart's gain.

(Jim Dooley, January 1987)

# No Opportunity for Preparation

Losing someone in completely unexpected circumstances gives
little immediate opportunity for beginning the task of grieving.
Utter disbelief at the news, even incredulous laughter, is by no
means uncommon. The idea of saying farewell to a loved one
for the day, only to be told later that same day that he or she
will never be coming back to us, is just too preposterous to
take in.

It is thought by many that crying is the only possible
immediate reaction:

'When I was told of Wendy's death, I thought, this is crazy.
I've just lost my wife; my children have no mother; but
how am I supposed to react? If this was a Hollywood film
production there would be close-ups of tear-stained faces. I
could not cry for two days; it was just impossible. I had to
force myself to look as if I was crying just for the benefit of
other people.'

There are no rules about when crying is acceptable and when
it is not, or when it should commence or cease. Only the person
who is grieving is entitled to be the judge of this.

There may be feelings of fear and insecurity and anger,

with periods of great intensity alternating with those of less intensity. Some days can be faced with more equanimity than others. This is the body's way of helping one to adjust, though, slowly and gradually. There may be feelings of detachment, as if one were not wholly present but standing apart, watching and noting one's every reaction:

'I was so exhausted by the physical response to grief that I felt as if I had temporarily left for a rest and was looking at this person who was me. I was intrigued at how I physically reacted to my emotions. I thought, "Right, the tears will soon be coming but not until after the multiple intakes of breath." I felt as if I was in a position to turn the whole thing off, like a television. But I couldn't, of course.'

Such reactions are indications that one is changing, in the sense of being propelled towards the next stage of one's life. There has been no chance to accept this inevitable change over a long period, thereby permitting a kinder adjustment. The change has been abrupt, brutal, the body needs to find a way of combating such brutality.

Of course, once the cold reality has been accepted, it will not make the task of grieving any easier, but it will enable the task of grieving to begin, when the mind and body are ready.

Releasing painful memories is something that will involve gradual change. For Lucy it meant coming to terms with very strong ambivalent feelings. She wanted to talk openly about her 'guilt'; she wanted to face up to her fear that she was to blame for her nephew's death, but agonized that by seeking to absolve herself from blame she might end up merely confirming and reinforcing her guilt. Nevertheless, she found the courage to explore her feelings and was later able to say:

'I have lost the person I was. I realize I am no longer that person. I have a need to grieve also for the person who is no longer the me that I recognize. I have to find a new identity. I have to move on somehow. I need to determine what my

87

expectations are. I realize I cannot go back to where I was before. I have a need to talk freely; to be open about it, so that I know exactly where I now stand. The more I talk the more I feel I am able to achieve that goal. It doesn't always feel like that immediately, but looking back I can see there has been a change for the better. I have had wonderful support.'

## Essential Support

Positive support in these circumstances is vital. The bereaved must not feel isolated and apologetic about reacting in a particularly intense or unpredictable way. Explosions of anger, perhaps even insulting and hurtful outbursts, are simply the uncontrollable expression of intense emotions which need an immediate outlet. His or her emotions may vary in intensity throughout this period.

It will be necessary to communicate with someone to whom one can relate; the very fact that one has begun to talk about it is an acknowledgement of some kind of acceptance, that one has set out on the road of grief. As already discussed, it is not always easy to find the right person for each individual's particular needs, and support groups can have a very important role to play in this respect. There is a wide variety of these, and their numbers are increasing. (A list of addresses will be found on page 207.)

## Learning

No matter what happens to us during our lifetime, we are always learning from our experiences. It may even be possible for a tragedy such as a death by accident to be viewed, in time, as not having been an *absolute* waste of a precious life. This is not to diminish the intensity of the loss, but it may be the case that some good can come out of the tragedy. For example, a vigorous campaign may be pursued by remaining loved ones in order to prevent a similar tragedy from happening to others. It may be some small compensation for such intense agony if the loss becomes the catalyst for a change or improvement in the quality of life for others.

Lucy's example is a case in point. Unable to accept that she was not to blame for the accident which killed her nephew she was encouraged to put her energies into something constructive, and joined a local pressure group which had been formed to lobby the county council to make roads in her neighbourhood safer for children. Her own tragic experience had given her a unique insight into the problem; she became a highly valued member of the executive committee, and a senior organizer of the publicity campaign with responsibility for both research and the preparation of press releases for the media. She had the idea of a newsletter to keep the community informed of progress, learned to use a word processor, and in due course became editor of the newsletter. After two years the pressure group was successful in its campaign; it also paved the way for improvements in other areas where similar dangers were identified.

The end of the campaign, though, did not mean the end of the organization. It adopted a watch-dog role and became a consultative group for other areas of community concern. Though the reason for her campaigning role will never be forgotten, Lucy's hurt and her heartache have been reduced, slowly.

Using one's own experiences to relate to people who find themselves in similar tragic situations can make an immense social and humanitarian contribution, in addition to helping the progress of one's own self-healing.

## SUICIDE

The loss of a loved one by an act that involves the taking of his or her own life cannot but compound the grief of the bereaved. In many cases a question will forever hang over the reason why the loved one chose to take this way out; the answer may never be found.

Thinking about suicide is not unusual; most people give it

a passing thought at least once in their lives. For the majority, though, it is just a transient thought that they have no intention of carrying out.

Very often it is assumed that the act of suicide is the result of a sudden experience so devastating that it cannot be tolerated. In reality suicide is rarely an impulsive act but rather something which has been privately contemplated over a long period. The actual decision to take one's own life will probably be provoked by an experience which has proved to be the final straw. What is particularly distressing about the act of suicide is the fact that the victim was unable to communicate his or her feelings of despair to anyone; the final decision was made alone, without any reference to anyone else.

Suicide is a statement about how one views one's life. One may feel that fulfilling certain expectations is impossible. Sometimes these expectations may be set unrealistically high as a result of personal ambition, or because of the demands of one's social surroundings. One considers oneself to be a failure, either through being too self-critical, or through having excessively low self-esteem. Sometimes happiness and personal fulfilment seem unattainable because one's sentiments are not reciprocated by others; there may be feelings of rejection; or inability to form any kind of relationship with other people. The act of self-dissolution, either as a result of anger or as a means of escape, therefore seems to be the only possible solution. Such a decision, though, it must be repeated, is never taken as a result of an isolated event. It is the coming together of many traumatic experiences into one tragic moment at which the risk of taking such action is at its highest.

## Reactions of Others

What are the reactions of those surrounding someone who has lost a loved one in this way? Do they view suicide in a different light from other ways of dying? How supportive and understanding are they likely to be? Given society's generally uninformed and fearful attitude to mental health, the answers to these questions are unlikely to be positive. Suicide is often regarded as something which is, at best, an embarrassment; at worst, something shameful. People are often discomfited at having known a suicide victim; the firm he worked for, or the clubs she used to go to, feel as if they might become tainted in some way by association. This attitude can have profound implications for those who have lost a loved one through suicide. The grieving process may be affected; the funeral service may feel different, and talking about it can be extremely difficult.

## A Shameful Death?

The unpredictable reactions of other people may inflict additional pain on the bereaved who may be made to feel emotionally suspect, as though they too are likely to be potential suicides. They may be made to feel different, or as though they were somehow on trial. People may avoid them out of fear of embarrassment, to the extent of making them feel ostracized. Worse still are explicit or implied accusations of blame, as though the bereaved were responsible in some way for what has happened:

'I was absolutely shattered at her reaction after Mum did it. She offered no help whatsoever during Mum's periodic bouts of depression; in fact, she seemed to go out of her way not to offer any help at all. Then she approached me one day and I thought perhaps I'd misjudged her after all, that was, until she opened her mouth. I have never heard such a torrent of abuse. She said, "I suppose you're glad now that Theresa's gone. Believe me, I know what she must have been going through, and you needn't play the innocent with me. Theresa was a good friend of mine years ago, but no one knows how their offspring will turn out. You have no conscience."

I couldn't offer any resistance to this shock onslaught. Until then it had never occurred to me that others might think that I somehow wanted, even helped, my mother to die.'

Such extremes, besides being grotesque, can only do harm, inculcating a desire in the bereaved to avoid people, and thus reducing their chances of finding the necessary empathetic help.

Having to face the world, then, can be almost as difficult as the task of grieving itself. It is no wonder that some are unable to accept the fact of suicide, and pretend that the cause of death was something else. Self-persuasion can result in a genuine belief in a false version of events, and to compensate for this the lost loved one can often become idealized to the point where true feelings are suppressed.

Family members who refuse to countenance the possibility of suicide, thereby deny themselves, and those others who wish to face the situation honestly, the mutual support which they need so much.

## A Case History: Mary

Mary was part of a strong Catholic family. Her mother and father were unable to face up to the fact of her sister's suicide: 'My parents practised their religion to the point where sin had to be excluded from the family. Minor transgressions were accepted, but we were always taught the error of our ways and that we should seek God's forgiveness at the next available confession. There's no doubt that on balance this was probably good for both my sister, Emma, and myself. It gave us a strong moral base to determine right from wrong as we were growing up.

'The little things, then, were alright, my parents could handle those. The real test came when Emma took the overdose. The inquest's verdict was suicide – there was no possibility of accident. I knew it and my parents knew it, but their reaction was to call the verdict a travesty, a mockery. They kept referring to "the accident" at first, but they knew what I was thinking. They just couldn't accept that their eldest daughter had, in their eyes, committed a mortal sin. Their only answer was to refuse to say anything. They never mentioned Emma unless it was to refer to "the accident". I can't tell you what this did to me. I don't even know what it has done to my parents, inside. They must be eaten away with a never-ending agony. If only they would face the truth. Don't they know God is supposed to forgive? Do they really think He is going to punish

Emma all over again? It has driven a wedge between us, ironically over the person we all loved.'

Insisting upon living a lie will only add to and prolong the period of grief. Trying to find a reason for such a tragedy and to undertake properly the task of grieving become impossible in the face of denial and the making up of falsehoods; the circle is unbreakable until the truth is accepted.

Attempting to gauge the reactions of outsiders may also be a cause for much worry. However, other people really must be left to their own conclusions, no matter what they are. Feelings of shame are utterly unnecessary; they exist only because of society's negative attitude, and will merely interfere with the task of grieving.

## Guilt

Never to really know why a loved one made that final decision is heart-breaking, and the bereaved are left to agonize over whether they could not have done something to prevent the tragedy. With hindsight they may feel that there were certain indications going back over a period, and that if they had intervened or sought help sooner, prevention might have been possible. They may feel that if they had been more patient, had paid more attention or shown more understanding, such a thing would not have happened.

Understandable as these feelings are, however, to assert that the situation could have been prevented by the remaining loved one is to suggest that the lost loved one must have been susceptible to great influence and control and that he or she could not have been in a position to make judgements and decisions for him or herself. Of course, there may be areas where it is properly felt that more help could have been offered, in retrospect, such as finding the time to hear what he or she had to say instead of making excuses about being 'too busy'. However, this must be placed in the context of the lost loved one's perception of his or her world. The reasons for him or her seeing it in a lethally distressing way are likely to be so complicated as to be virtually impossible to determine. To convince oneself that certain gestures by the remaining loved one may have halted an act of self-dissolution is to profoundly underestimate the power of the human psyche.

In the usual parent and child relationship, for example, are not children always wanting to make their own decisions and wanting to get away from parental control, albeit not necessarily by physically leaving home? They *want* control over their own lives and this will mean letting them make decisions for themselves. Surely it is unrealistic, therefore, to take the view that, in the suicide of a loved one, things could not have had such a tragic ending if just a little more care, understanding or love had been shown?

## The Possibility of Repetition?

The death of a loved one by suicide can sometimes leave survivors with the fear that they may be susceptible to the same kinds of feelings which led up to the self-destructive decision.

The idea sometimes expressed that suicide runs in families is considered to be unfounded and unjust, whatever the occasional pattern of events may suggest. If such a thing does recur, it is likely to be the result of the family's failure to acknowledge the original tragedy and talk frankly about it, with the result that other family members may subconsciously feel that suicide is somehow an acceptable way out. A negative example has been set, and there has been no opportunity in the intervening period in which to learn how to come to terms with the tragedy and to release pent-up feelings. Talking openly and truthfully is vital, especially amongst family members, to allay any fears of repetition.

## The Need to Say Goodbye

It is very often the case that suicide victims seem the unlikeliest of people ever to take their own lives. Having been given no inkling, those left behind may feel they never had the opportunity to offer comfort or advice, or to understand what was troubling their loved one so profoundly, let alone a chance to say goodbye.

## A Case History: Jane

Jane and Peter are teachers; they had been shouldering the responsibility for helping Jane's sister, Susan, through the stressful period of her divorce. Jane telephoned her father to ask his advice: 'I asked him to have a quiet word with Susan. We were sure this would help my sister as they had always been very close. I never expected any reaction other than one of total concern. What greeted me was a complete shock. He answered me in a way I had never heard him speak before.

'I hadn't see him for about three months as he was up north on some business. The last time we met he seemed fine, there was no indication of there being anything on his mind; but, phoning him this time was like taking a cork out of a bottle of champagne. Susan seemed furthest from his mind. He just kept saying that he had had enough, that there seemed no point to anything any more and that he couldn't possibly be of any help to anyone. He talked of the dreadful pressure he was under, but I didn't really know what he meant. He seemed so distraught. I tried to console him and he seemed to calm down quite a bit. When I put the phone down I just thought he was having terrible business problems. He had had them before but they had never been anything to worry about for long.

'Daddy was found three days later. He had left a suicide note that stated only where he wanted to be buried. I was in a state of shock. I had just had no idea how bad he must have been feeling. How much had he suffered all these years? Why didn't he tell us before? Why didn't I realize something was so terribly wrong? Oh, how I needed to ask him face to face and to put my arms around him and to tell him I loved him. I just clammed up. I couldn't share my feelings with anyone. I just couldn't talk about it and I felt so awful inside.

'This went on for about three months until someone realized my heart-break and approached me. I allowed myself to be persuaded to do something that I thought was pretty awful at first. It was suggested to me that I might try writing a letter to Daddy. How could I write a letter to someone who cannot possibly read it, I thought? I did, however. I tried hard to put into it what I wanted

95

to say to him, how I felt I had been denied the chance of telling him my feelings for him. It was the hardest thing I ever did in my life. I didn't get very far at first and I gave up several times because my emotions just seemed to run away with me. His note left so many questions unanswered . . . Why should he have wanted to so it? Did he feel deserted by us all?

'I did finally manage to write that letter. It was a wonder I could see what I was doing, what with the tears, and it took ages. But I put down everything I felt, even the tiniest detail. Nothing was left out. A part of me had been put into words. I knew he could never read it, but the fact that I had written the letter somehow gave me the feeling that he would know what I was saying. I felt as if I had communicated my feelings to him. It was a tremendous relief.

'What I said was very, very private. It is not possible to share those thoughts with anyone other than Daddy, and I'm sure he now knows how I feel.'

## Telling Children

Telling children of the death of a loved one is a difficult area, particularly in the case of a suicide. There may be a natural tendency to want to protect children from the truth, but there are only two alternatives: half-truths and lies. And whilst immediate family members may decide to censor the truth, children go to school, they meet friends, and at some time or other they are bound to find out. In any case children can be quick to detect unease or furtiveness on the part of adults, they will suspect something is being kept from them, and the deception cannot be sustained for long.

It is not suggested that a full revelation should be made all at once. A situation which has such a profoundly disturbing effect on adults is likely to affect a child in a similar way. However, they should be told, in a way which is appropriate for the circumstances. They should be allowed to ask questions, and they should receive honest answers.

## A Case History: Ellen

Ellen was nine when her mother committed suicide. She was told that her mother had gone to heaven because she had been feeling very, very tired. She was now resting peacefully and was happy. The true nature of the tragedy was successfully kept from Ellen for nearly ten years, partly due to the fact that the family moved to the other end of the country shortly after the tragedy.

Ellen had accepted the reasons given for her mother's death. However, in due course she gained a place at a university not far from the village where she had lived as a child and where her mother had died. She decided to revisit the place, and it was during the course of the most casual of conversations in the village shop that Ellen discovered that her mother had hanged herself. This was confirmed when she obtained a copy of her mother's death certificate.

That official paper with its cold, clinical statement conveyed nothing to Ellen of her mother's reasons for her desperate action. She felt a void had opened up. A void between herself and her family, whom she felt had cheated her all these years by not telling her the truth. A void between herself and her mother. The parent whose memory she had cherished all these years was now a different person.

Ellen's trauma began. She felt unable to continue her university studies and left after a poor initial six months. She experienced weight and hair loss. She spent a very long time mourning anew the loss of her mother and looking into her mother's life and death, and re-examining her own life, before she reached the point where a fresh beginning seemed possible. With time and empathetic support she came to terms with the reasons why her family had tried to protect her from the truth, and became reconciled, especially to her father, from whom she had felt most alienated. For their part, the family began to see how Ellen's needs had been allowed to suffer. A new chapter began for all of them, based now on honesty and mutual support.

Despite Ellen's acceptance and reconciliation, she still feels a sense of deprivation which leaves her with a degree of sadness. The damage done by not knowing the truth for those ten years, she feels, can never be fully repaired, and though it is now bearable, the pain will never leave her.

Ellen's story shows how being economical with the truth can well cause a double burden of grief. Having come to terms with the death of a loved one as a child only to learn the truth about that death later will give rise to a new period of grief.

The lies that have been accepted as truth have to be discarded, and a new set of facts has to be grasped, changing one's entire perspective on the loved one and on one's own life.

Without honest answers to their questions, children can easily feel that they are somehow to blame, especially if the lost loved one's name is seldom mentioned for fear of provoking more questions. A child will only ask questions about that which he or she can grasp. To try to deceive them is to underestimate them as intelligent, caring beings. They, too, have a need to talk, to be listened to, and to be allowed to mourn.

The full implication of a death may not be apparent to a child. The concept of blame is relatively easy for children to understand; the concept of dying is not. Without having an adequate grasp of why Mummy or Daddy are no longer able to be with them, for example, children can easily blame themselves, feeling they must have done something terrible for their parents no longer to want to be near them.

Telling a child the truth will not be easy. The alternative, however, is unthinkable.

# 7   The Loss of a Child

The loss of a child is perhaps the kind of death that is most feared and most agonized over, if one is forced to categorize. Children are a part of their parents in a way that extends far beyond what can be described as bonding. Although losing a parent is profoundly distressing, it is usually perceived as being the natural order. Parents do not expect to outlive their children. Children are their link with future generations. The death of a child cuts off all expectations, and future hopes and dreams are thrown into turmoil.

## From the Beginning

The death of a child is the loss of the person whom the parents have helped create. That individual's life was perceived and planned by his or her mother and father and began with an act of mutual physical and emotional love between them. The feelings of attachment by a woman to the foetus and the unborn baby it becomes is probably much greater for her, being the result of her pregnancy, than it is for the more passively roled father. The act of carrying a child in the womb, by definition, places a woman in much closer proximity to the developing baby than is the case with the father. This physical closeness, this life-sustaining dependency, is also likely to place a woman in much closer emotional contact with her baby during this time. The movements the unborn child will make inside its mother can have an effect which can only be guessed at by the father. The human male's attachment to the life which he has helped to create, probably becomes as intense as the mother's only from the moment he is able to see, touch and hold that newly born life.

# A LESSER BEREAVEMENT?

People who have lost a child because of a miscarriage, still-birth, or neo-natal death are often considered to be in a lesser category of bereavement than those who are regarded as being in a position to establish a meaningful bond with their child. They are encouraged to 'try again' and to 'put it all behind them', as though the trauma were a minor mishap rather than a bereavement. Such attitudes prevail only in people who have never experienced such heartache. Their callousness is not intentional; it stems from an inability to understand what this means to the parents, and ignorance of what to say or do that might offer comfort. They feel embarrassed; they had probably been looking forward to the birth, too; they may already have offered gifts; now, they simply do not know what to say. There may be a feeling that the event is too close to home; they may not want to be reminded of what could happen to their children. Such platitudes as 'It is probably for the best' bring no comfort to the bereaved parents, and serve no useful purpose.

## Sudden Infant Death Syndrome

This is also known as cot death, and despite many theories its cause remains a mystery. The tragic reality is that a perfectly healthy baby can be placed in the cot in perfectly normal circumstances, only to discover that death has occurred some time later from no apparent cause.

## What Did We Do That Was So Wrong?

There may well be an inclination on the part of the parents to blame themselves. It is quite possible that the death has had to be reported to the coroner and that there has been an inquest. The police and social workers may have been involved, all of which serves to make the parents of a SIDS victim suffer increased feelings of guilt. They may feel that their suitability as parents is in question. Siblings, too, may blame themselves, wondering if they loved the baby enough. The reaction of a baby-sitter may also be one of self-blame.

Parents may feel victimized after an initial misdiagnosis, and their tragedy is compounded by the prospect of being labelled as social deviants. Thankfully, however, with an increasing public awareness of the existence of cot death this label is now less readily applied by others, especially professionals. The bluish, leaden colour on the body which can be apparent following a baby's demise, and which could be mistaken for bruising, is now recognized as being an effect of SIDS.

## The Need for Support

The loss of an infant through 'cot death' is quite likely to be a couple's first experience of bereavement, especially when the parents concerned are relatively young. Their friends and acquaintances are likely to be similarly inexperienced and may feel, therefore, that they are not in a position to help or they may simply not want to help. There may also be feelings still by others that carelessness, even neglect, has somehow contributed towards the tragedy. Consequently, all these factors may be a reason for the dearth of support for those who are having to face such a loss. Traditional providers of support during bereavement may be lacking and the parents concerned may feel they are faced with having to cope by themselves.

This is particularly inequitable when one considers that support may be particularly necessary in a 'cot death' bereavement. The parents may continually be reproaching themselves, perhaps even reproaching each other by questioning the performance of their respective partners as mother or father. He may be wondering if his wife has been administering proper care during his working hours. She may be wondering if her husband handled the baby with sufficient care. Alternatively, each may be thinking that this is the other's opinion of him or her. Such absence of positive support can be distressing and possibly damaging in the long term.

With specialized counselling there will be no pressure to get over the loss, and there will be the opportunity to talk openly about feelings of guilt and blame without the constraints of family or friends. The parents can talk about the baby, who was so much a part of their relationship, as a real person who is loved and desperately missed, and not be made to feel that their infant's existence was too short-lived to be important or urged to forget and move on.

It is also important to examine feelings of guilt and mutual recriminations and self-blame in the light of a coroner's verdict. Has any blame been imputed by the decision? Has there been criticism of the way in which care was given? Even if feelings of self-blame are still experienced, it should not be assumed that there is no option other than to live with them. A good GP or consultant paediatrician should be willing to discuss the circumstances surrounding the death. It will then be possible to make a comparison with other cases of SIDS, thereby enabling parents to gradually reduce their feelings of guilt. The Foundation for the Study of Infant Deaths may be a source of help to bereaved parents (address on page 209).

## CULPABILITY

The initial feeling of parents who have lost a child that blame must somehow attach to them for what has happened, is almost universal. After all, they feel, they were in control of the child's life and therefore they must take the blame for the tragedy. There may be a thousand reasons for the accident, but the parents will hold themselves responsible for what has happened.

In Chapter 6, the account of Lucy's tragedy was given. Despite the fact that Lucy was driving the car that killed Stephen, Stephen's mother and father still could not avoid blaming themselves for what had happened:

'I was Stephen's mother. I told him time and time again not to open the front garden gate and go out into the road, but why was I so naïve in not realizing that boys will be boys? I ought to have made sure he was safe and got that gate fixed. I was with him all day and it's my fault. I am to blame and I don't know how I'm going to live with it.'

'As Stephen's father, I am head of the house. I know my wife and I are equal partners, but, ultimately, I feel responsible for the safety of my family. My family is devastated and I am to blame. I held my sister-in-law, Lucy, to blame in the most terrible way at first, but now I realize I was just abdicating *my* responsibilities. I cannot escape the fact that I placed my son's life second to saving money by not getting the fencing repaired.'

## Is Guilt Avoidable?

It is probably true to say that guilt arising from the loss of a son or daughter is unavoidable. Such feelings can perhaps be considered as an extension of the love that was felt during the child's brief lifetime. They are the expression of a need to have the child back, to embrace it and keep it safe in one's arms forever. The impossibility of satisfying this need is heart-breaking; feeling guilt is a mjor outlet for such an overwhelming need. In the absence of the loved one, the only way to express one's love is by shouldering almost obligatory feelings of culpability.

These feelings must be recognized as a part of one's grief. How long they will last will depend upon the individual but they will not last forever. To overcome them, however, it is essential to face up to them.

## Dealing with Guilt

Talking to those who have lost a child is hard enough. For bereaved parents to talk about their loss to others, it may be even harder. It really is immensely difficult for someone who has not lost a child to comprehend the feelings of those who have. Consequently, there can be a wall of silence encircling the death. It must be realized from the outset, however, that the circle, unless broken, will become larger and larger and will appear more and more troublesome. The important point is to recognize this inevitability and to seek to end it.

It must be understood that it is likely nothing could have reasonably been done to have halted such a tragedy. Think, for example, of the many thousands of children who make their way to school each day. Think of the many dangers that they face in a modern society. Is it really reasonable to suppose that a tragedy could have been prevented from occurring from any one of these things? Reducing the chances of such a tragedy occurring may be considered possible but this would have to be at the expense of reasonable liberty and few children are going to be tolerable to live with if a degree of basic freedom is to be denied to them.

Also, it could be argued that being too restrictive will encourage children to make the most productive use of freedom, when allowed, which could only heighten such dangers and, consequently, possibly increase the risk of such a tragedy occurring.

The conclusion must be that it is not a reasonable expectation that intervention and prevention are always possible. Feelings of intense guilt can only be truly justifiable where there is a consistently cavalier attitude to one's children; not caring where they are at any time of the day or night. In such circumstances, though, there is likely to be the irony of such parents *not* experiencing guilt to the same degree, if at all.

Those who have lost a child through congenital illness may feel that it should not have been conceived. And yet that child has experienced the joy of loving parents during its brief life; the strength and courage to accommodate his or her condition owes much to the parents, and sharing that young life has been enriching for everyone. The tragedy now being faced involves a great deal of pain and anguish, but it should not mean having to endure guilt and self-reproach.

## SUPPORT

It is particularly necessary for the bereaved to seek empathetic relationships. It is vital for parents to be allowed to talk freely and for as long as they need about their loss. They need others to say how special their child was, and how much he or she meant to other people. They need to be reassured about the care and love they gave to that child.

They may be thankful for extra attention shown to a surviving brother or sister, especially in the early stages. They will not want to hear that they can 'try again'; they do not need advice on how to get over their loss quickly.

Consequently, it is particularly important for those who have suffered the loss of a child to secure help from others who have been through a similar experience, and who will provide support for as long as it is needed. There is no necessity to try to cope alone: support groups are flourishing; a list of useful addresses appears on page 207.

## CHILDREN AND GRIEF

The remaining child or children should never be regarded as being in need of protection from the truth. It must not be supposed that grief in children can be reduced or eliminated.

The concept of death in very young children is absent or very limited. However, they can conceive of guilt and they may feel that they are responsible for what has happened. This is especially true of children between the ages of six and ten, and those in this age group must be reassured that there is no basis for their anxiety. They should be treated as persons in their own right and be allowed to participate in a shared knowledge of death.

Children's thoughts about death depend very much on the stage of development they have reached. In her study, 'The Child's Theories Concerning Death'. Maria Nagy indicated three stages of understanding. Briefly, these are: between the ages of three and five, where death cannot be seen as a final end to life – it is only temporary; between the ages of five and nine, where death becomes symbolized as a person, and only those people die who are carried away by the death person – such a 'person' being kept remote from themselves; however, from the age of nine onwards, the concept of death as they will understand it for the rest of their lives becomes recognized.

Siblings should be allowed to see their little sister or brother after death, but this should not be forced upon them if they are patently distressed at the prospect. However, any tendency for adults to recoil at the idea of children seeing the body of a lost loved one may be doing them a complete disservice, and may well foster the idea that death is something to be ashamed of or to feel guilty about. Young children, it should be remembered, are likely to misinterpret casual euphemisms. The concept of someone having gone away or gone to sleep is something that is understood only in its usual, everyday form, and therefore will be strictly applied to what they see and what they are told. Consequently, quite unnecessary distress can be caused.

Similarly, there is little reason to deny a child the chance to attend the funeral. In Chapter 1, Edward's story showed how his parents' attempts to protect him from the processes of death and dying became almost absurd, and were counter-productive. Children are permitted to have their own form of funeral service for pets, so why do some adults feel it is necessary to protect them from the real thing?

The section 'Telling Children' (page 96) in Chapter 6 examines further this important issue.

## THE DYING CHILD

A child who is dying may initially realize something is wrong by the change in his or her parents' behaviour. They may seem more tolerant, more generous and protective, and less concerned to find fault.

Age and experience are likely to play an important part in a child's understanding of how she or he is dying. A baby under the age of one year will have no perception of its own situation or that its parents have begun grieving for him or her, although, the changed way in which its parents are reacting may well give rise to vexation. The way a dying baby is given special attention by its parents, however, is likely

106

to be perceived as being nothing other than normal. In fact, a perfectly healthy baby is likely to have similar feelings to those of a dying baby.

The perceptions of children under the age of four years are based on their understanding of situations immediately facing them. For example, the child confined to hospital may well experience the same feelings of parental alienation as a healthy child who experiences a parental absence from the home. Both can experience comparable feelings of bereavement.

Young children over the age of four will gradually be aware of wider implications, and will not be content to see situations in isolation. Parental reactions and activities seen to be associated with the child's physical condition may well cause them concern and provoke such questions as 'Why do mummy and daddy keep blowing their nose or rubbing their eyes'.

Children over the age of nine will begin to grasp the concept of dying and their own mortality and are likely to ask more direct questions. However, these age divisions are only generalizations and a dying child of very tender years may be as aware of his or her condition as one much older. In *New Meanings of Death*, Myra Bluebond-Langer states that the ability to 'integrate and synthesize information' is experience-related rather than age-related. She describes three- and four-year olds of average intelligence who knew more about their progress than very intelligent nine-year olds, the reason being the degree of experience of serious illness the younger children had had.

A dying child, then, is likely to be alert to his or her changed situation and will detect a less-than-honest attitude by parents and others. Adults, whether family or professionals, can easily underestimate a child's grasp of the situation. They may assume that a child will only understand what is happening if an explanation is given, whereas Myra Bluebond-Langer in *The Private Worlds of Dying Children* shows that critically ill and dying children are often far more aware of their own condition than adults are prepared to admit.

This is the time when getting to know one's child as a *person* is really possible. It is a time for being together as equals and preparing the paths of grief for each other. However, this can only be achieved if honesty is allowed to prevail. Gently answering the questions that will be asked, and in a way that allows assimilation and eventual acceptance, is an important consideration both for the dying child and for those who are to become bereaved.

This is not to overlook the fear of dying that a child may have. This fear may be so great that there is a strong desire to deny that he or she has only a short time to live. As with adults, there may be a refusal to have anything to do with procedures perceived as being concerned with the sustaining of life. There may be anger or silence; a refusal to talk about the future, or concern that things be done immediately. In a situation such as this, the natural defence mechanism of death-rejection must be seen as a starting point, as a spring-board to a full communicating relationship where such major fears can be identified and allowed to be voiced, implicitly or explicitly, to an empathetic listener. Observing fears and anxieties may be possible during periods of recreation and play. Such emotions may also be evident in drawings, and the clues provided during such activities can provide the opportunity for a meaningful talk. It may be the case that the child will only confide his or her intimate thoughts to certain people, and certainly coercion should never be used in bringing such fears into the open. However, the knowledge that talking will not be met with a wall of silence or rejection may provide the stimulus for questions and answers.

Once a dialogue has been established apprehensions may begin to be dispelled and, given time and patience, much can be achieved. Overcoming non-communication and its attendant emotional loneliness can bring a dying child nearer to peace. Knowing that nothing which is felt needs to be hidden can play a major part in easing the path of grief for that child.

Great fortitude and forbearance is sometimes shown by children who are dying and are now trying to accept the inevitable. The impending end to their lives can fill them with great compassion and concern for others, and can even bestow upon them a marvellous sense of humour. It can also be a time when reassurances are sought about how much they are loved *for themselves*, despite the faults which they know they possess. Acceptance of themselves by their loved ones can bring out feelings of immense closeness in dying children. The consequence of such feelings can be physically and emotionally enriching for everyone, and may even leave parents who are or have been in such a situation at a spiritual advantage over those who have not.

# 8  The Loss of a Baby

by Rita Fraser

Whenever someone we love dies, we go through a period of grief and mourning and this is a very natural and necessary process. The death of a loved and hoped-for baby is no less a bereavement and yet the effects of this loss are sometimes misunderstood and frequently underestimated.

The loss of a baby is a very special sort of bereavement; some would say that it is one of the worst. When a loved friend, relative or spouse dies there is, of course, pain, shock and great sadness, but this may be tempered, eventually, by memories of happier times together. There are usually others around who knew that person and who share both the memories and the grief. When a baby dies during pregnancy, at birth, or soon afterwards, there is a terrible feeling of emptiness; a loss of future hopes and dreams; of expected joys; and this can lead to a terrible loneliness. People may think that because the child never lived, it had no real existence at all and this can be very painful for the parents to bear. After all, they have nurtured, loved, planned for, even built a future around that baby. It can be very difficult to explain to friends and family that your baby was very much alive for you.

We all take pregnancy and childbirth for granted and we are led to expect a healthy baby at the end of it. When something goes wrong it is a shattering blow. There are often few tangible memories to hold on to – and most of them are shared only by the parents. There is the excitement when it is realized that a new life is being carried; the thrill of seeing your child as it turns somersaults on an ultrasound screen; those first fluttering movements; the nightly routine of kicks and thumps the minute you try to sleep. Then, suddenly, all you have is a still, cold baby son or daughter, seen and held for such a short time, instead of a warm new life and the first cries that herald the change from partnership to family. There

110

may be a photograph, a lock of hair, a tiny coffin, a posy of flowers and a name in a Book of Remembrance. There are never the congratulations and cards; the gifts of baby clothes and matinée coats; the proud grandparents arriving at the hospital; the sense of having fulfilled one's role as a woman and having joined that exclusive club, motherhood.

Instead, there are empty arms; milk that is not needed; no nurse carrying a shawl-wrapped baby to the car; an empty house; a silent nursery; a cot to dismantle; clothes to pack away and all too often the silence and embarrassment of others who do not know how to handle this particular kind of bereavement and who cross the road to avoid you rather than risk you bursting into tears. However, hardest of all is the realization that nobody else knew the tiny person that you have lost and as a result of whose death you feel that life has no meaning. It is a dream, or rather a nightmare, but one from which you know you will not wake.

## MISCARRIAGE

Miscarriage is often regarded by both the medical profession and the general public as a comparatively trivial event and one which the woman should rapidly come to terms with. The reality is that although it may not be physically life-threatening (although it can be painful), the shock and sadness that follow are out of proportion to the actual event. Although miscarriage is very common and medically routine, it is no less devastating when it happens to you. People may find your sadness difficult to understand when the pregnancy was so short-lived. This can make you feel guilty. However, you cannot and should not measure grief according to the number of weeks' pregnancy. At the time, there is no greater grief than your own, it is only much later that you can look beyond it.

Perhaps one of the worst aspects of miscarriage is the intangibility of it all. You must mourn a baby of unknown sex which has never been seen or named, and this can add to the sense of unreality. There is no grave to visit or to put flowers on, neither is there any photograph to prove that you really did have a baby. However long that baby was carried, it is a real person to you. From the minute you knew you were pregnant you had planned a future for that child; given it a name and looked forward to it growing up. After a miscarriage you leave the hospital feeling empty and bewildered, with absolutely nothing to show for it. When you get home, the attitude of those around you may cause even more pain, with such comments as 'It was for the best', or 'You can always have another one' or 'There must have been something wrong with it'. While rationally you know all of these things, emotionally you still need to grieve. Believing a baby to be abnormal does not always lessen the sadness. You need time to grieve and to adjust to that loss.

## STILLBIRTH

Stillbirth is a complete and utter shock. An event which was to have caused such joy suddenly becomes a nightmare. Death has no place in the process of birth, the natural order of things is turned upside down. Instead of welcoming new life into the world, there is a funeral to prepare for.

If the baby dies *in utero*, the mother must still go through all the pain of labour knowing that she will not have a living baby at the end of it. She may not even believe that it is true and may cling to the belief, right up until the last minute, that the doctors are wrong; that the heart monitors and scanning machines are faulty; that it is just a mistake and that the baby will, somehow, be born alive and well. She may not feel that she can face the labour ahead of her and she may ask for a Caesarean to be performed so as to eliminate any awareness of birth until it is all over. However, a Caesarian is rarely performed, except for medical reasons, because of the need to maximize the prospects of having a healthy baby at a later date. It is also better for the woman herself to be aware of what is going on, otherwise she may have difficulty in accepting that the baby has died.

# NEO-NATAL DEATH

If a baby dies in a Special Care Baby Unit, the time leading up to the baby's death is very important. Sometimes parents have been unable to hold their baby because of all the paraphernalia surrounding their child. They may be frightened of how death will occur and become overawed by all the technology. It is important to have sensitive staff around to answer questions and to offer reassuring presence, if required.

After hours or days of not knowing whether the baby will live or die, and watching a tiny son or daughter fighting for life, there may be a sense of relief that the uncertainty is finally over and that the baby is no longer in any pain or discomfort. When it is recognized that the baby is dying, it may be removed from all or some of the support systems, so that the parents can hold it without being encumbered by all the various items of equipment. One mother wrote:

'Up until then we hadn't been able to hold him. They got him out and wrapped him up and passed him to me. How I will treasure those few precious moments of holding him. After a couple of minutes he started to gasp. I found it distressing and passed him to my husband, but I think he may already have died by then. It was the first time I had ever seen my husband cry, as he held our little bundle. He looked such a natural father. Looking back I wish I had had more courage and held him longer, but I suppose no length of time would have been long enough.'

# TERMINATION FOR FOETAL ABNORMALITY

With the advent of sophisticated equipment for pre-natal testing such as ultrasound, amniocentesis and chorion biopsy, a new form of bereavement faces some parents; that of terminating a pregnancy where a baby is found to be severely abnormal.

113

It can be a devastating experience to discover half-way through a pregnancy considered to be normal that a baby is going to be born with a severe handicap, or might die before, during or soon after birth. At first, there may be utter disbelief and a hope that doctors have made a mistake. Later, there may be a feeling of anger and of wanting to get rid of the baby as soon as possible. Parents may feel very alone in their grief, knowing that they have made a decision to terminate a much-wanted baby. Guilt may be particularly strong, because it has been their decision alone. The woman may be torn between the desire to carry on with the pregnancy at all costs and the realization that she could not cope with a severely abnormal baby, so that for her sake and her family's she must agree to a termination. The parents may find it difficult to talk to anyone else because of the feeling that everybody is judging them and criticizing their decision, yet they will be going through all the feelings of grief and loss which are produced by any other kind of bereavement. They will miss and long for their baby in the same way as other bereaved parents, yet all the time they may feel an overriding sense of guilt at having conceived a handicapped baby, and at having decided to terminate the pregnancy.

There may be a great sense of failure at having conceived a less than perfect baby and a fear of future pregnancies ending in the same way. All this can lead to parents withdrawing into themselves, because they feel that no one else will understand their decision. They may not even be able to talk to each other about their true feelings, particularly if one partner was more reluctant to proceed with the termination.

It is important that such parents are prepared for the labour and birth that is to take place and that they are given the same opportunities to see, hold and name their baby, if they wish. Photographs should be taken and kept on file if the parents feel they do not want them at the time. The question of disposal should also be discussed in case parents should wish to arrange a funeral, rather than leaving such a decision to the hospital.

Most importantly, parents should be encouraged to talk over their loss, rather than bottling it up, and here a support group such as SATFA (Support After Termination of Foetal Abnormality) (see page 211 for address) may be able to put them in touch with other parents who have been through this traumatic loss.

## THE GRIEF PROCESS

When one loses a baby, at whatever stage of pregnancy, the feelings are very similar to any other form of bereavement. Different emotions may come and go; some may be very intense, others comparatively fleeting. You may swing from one mood to another. Everybody is different and responds to the situation in a unique way. However, there are certain stages which most people do go through, to a greater or lesser extent. Yet we must eventually emerge from our grief and pick up the pieces of our lives. There is no time limit on how long the healing will take – it would be foolish to promise that someone will feel better in a month, or six months, or a year. But little by little healing *does* take place and we will realize that, in time, a minute, then an hour, then a day will go by when we have not thought about our lost baby. The good days gradually outshine the bad days. Imperceptibly, and without us having to do anything specific, we will realize that the future can be faced. Not that our babies will be forgotten or replaced like an outgrown dress. There is an inclination towards accepting what has been and what will be. We cannot change what has happened, but we can use our experience to grow. Through the love and support of our partners, families and friends, we can move on with courage and hope.

At first one may be in a state of shock and disbelief. The whole experience can seem like a dream. There is overwhelming grief and a feeling of loss and devastation. There may be tears, or there may be a state of numbness, as if it is all happening to someone else. Tears can be a good way of releasing the tension and sadness and can help one on the road to recovery, although, it must be said, some people are not able to cry easily. Family and friends may pose a problem in that they may not know how to react when you do cry. They may feel embarrassed and not want to talk about your baby in case it upsets you. But tears are natural and normal.

It is at this initial stage that some women wish that they,too, had died. Even the thought of how much their husband and other children need them cannot reduce this desire to join their baby.

There may be feelings of anger and bitterness that this child has been taken away from you. You may blame doctors, nurses, midwives, God, your husband or yourself. You may ask whether anything more could have been done to save the baby. Parents often feel guilty and wonder where they went wrong and why such a dreadful thing has happened and what could have been done to prevent it. The questions are endless and the answers elusive, leading to feelings of failure and inadequacy – 'What is it that enables other women to achieve with ease that which I cannot achieve at all?' To lose a baby often means losing one's confidence. The questions 'Why me?' and 'What have I done to deserve this?' are very common. It seems so unfair and such a waste of everything.

Jealousy can also be a problem. It may seem that some women have numerous children which they apparently do not want, whilst others are unable to manage one live baby. Some women cannot bear to see another baby. For others, it is the sight of a pregnant woman that causes them most anguish. Some desperately need to hold a baby, not to replace the one that has been lost, but to fill their empty, aching arms (this feeling of emptiness is often said to resemble a physical pain). Here a sensitive friend or relative may help but letting the mother that was to be hold it and even weep over it, if that is going to be a comfort to her. It may be possible, in hospital, for a woman to be brought another baby to hold (with the mother's permission, of course) for a short time. Although staff may be uneasy at the prospect of handling such a situation, it is said by most women who have experienced this to be a great comfort to them, besides confirming to themselves that it is their own baby they long for and not someone else's.

One of the worst feelings is sense of isolation. It can seem as if one is alone in grief but with a desperate need to talk about the experience. Some women are shocked by the range of emotions they feel, many of which seem totally out of character. It can come as a surprise to find that one is wishing that a similar disaster would befall close friends or family members, so that they might glean some idea of one's suffering. Depression is evident in many women and this can lead to a lack of interest in the future. Sleep may be difficult at such a time and when sleep is possible, nightmares about the lost baby may be experienced.

The most common feeling and, perhaps, the most misunderstood, is the irreplaceable nature of the lost baby. For however long that baby has been carried, it is a very real person to you, but people often do not realize that you want the baby you have lost and not just another one. Untold hurt can be caused by insensitive remarks such as 'Never mind, you are young, you can always have another'. You *do* mind and, besides, you will probably be lacking in sufficient confidence to envisage risking the trauma of another pregnancy. Nobody would think of comforting a newly-bereaved widow with the words 'Don't worry, you can always find another husband!'. Yet people seem to think that a baby is easily replaced.

Those with children already may receive comments reflecting this fact. Although it is comforting to know that one has other children, it does not diminish the intensity of the loss. It can often be harder, in fact, knowing exactly what you are missing. As one mother wrote following the birth of her son, after she had lost her three previous babies late in pregnancy:

'I still cannot get over how much I love him. It's just overwhelming. I'm almost grateful for not having a baby before losing the others. I'm sure it would have been so much harder to have known what I was losing.'

Some women feel resentment towards their children for, as they see it, intruding on their grief. The need to work through their sorrow is considered sacrificed because of the necessity of maintaining a daily routine, giving them little time for private grief. However, such feelings are usually transient. Nevertheless, it may help the parents if they are allowed to spend some time together, alone, providing there is an understanding person to look after the remaining children.

As time progresses, a woman may feel that she is in a kind of time-warp, in which she is locked into her grief whilst others all around her, it seems, have moved their emotions on a stage or two and are resuming their normal lives. This can feel extremely hurtful, as it appears to her that nobody cares any more and that they have forgotten the baby already. As one woman wrote:

'I sat staring out of the window, watching all the people going about their daily business, oblivious to what had happened to me. I wanted to scream at them, to let them know that my baby had died and how could they carry on as if they simply didn't care!'

It may be some time before a woman is able to stop seeing her life in terms of a failed pregnancy – 'I would have been thirty-six weeks by now ... Today would have been my scan ... The baby should have been born, today' – all such milestones must be reached and mourned over. Some women find that the first anniversary of the baby's birth and death is a very traumatic time. In some ways, it is a relief to get it over with and it can seem easier once this date has passed. It may even be an anticlimax when it does eventually arrive.

Along with all the other guilt feelings, some parents may experience guilt about grieving for their baby when other people seem to have much worse problems. Indeed, some people may try to foster this feeling in you by seeking to compare your loss with that of others, in the hope that it might help. However, grief cannot be measured against someone else's tragedy. One's pain will not be any less because others think that their grief is worse. There is no greater loss than one's own, at the time. It is only much later that it is possible to look beyond one's own grief and to find some kind of perspective.

118

# THE GRIEF OF THE FATHER

When a baby is lost, the father may feel very frustrated and powerless. He may desperately want to help his partner, but it is she who must go through the physical pain of childbirth. It is usually left to him to inform friends and relatives of the death of the baby and to organize the formal arrangements surrounding the bereavement. For the sake of others, he is expected to be strong and not to show his feelings too much. He may feel obliged to conform to society's expectations that men do not express their emotions, and this can make it very difficult, even impossible, for the man to vent his grief properly. This is notwithstanding that a man may feel as much devastation and sadness as his partner, but he may be unable to share such feelings with her.

Men often say that they feel left out of the whole grieving process, because the first concern of friends and relatives is usually the welfare of the mother. Yet a man's needs ought to be recognized. As one father, Ben, wrote:

'I confess that there were times when, as visitors crowded around Judith, I felt left out, or wished that my own feelings could have been given franker recognition. I felt myself retreating within myself and, at times, descending into shocked inner silence. Eventually, I developed mouth ulcers, mimicking Richard's bilateral cleft palate, and my temperature went chaotic. I found myself grieving for the loss of *my* son.'

If partners are unable to share their grief together, this can lead to problems later. Women frequently say that it seems as if their husband no longer cares, that he has recovered from his loss and has been able to pick up the pieces of his life so quickly. This can be very frustrating for the mother, who is often desperate to talk about the loss, over and over again. There *is* a difference in the way men and women grieve. Whilst the woman may cry easily and frequently, the man may only cry at the time of the loss, or perhaps at the funeral

119

or maybe not at all. In her delicate emotional state, the woman may interpret this as a sign that her partner does not care.

Some fathers even find it difficult to mention the baby by name, simply changing the subject if his partner starts talking about the child, or suddenly remembering that there is something important to do.

It is often assumed that great tragedy will bring a couple closer together and for some this is undeniably true. However, when a baby dies the grief of both parents may be so great that they are simply unable to support each other. It can be a great shock to find that at a time when you thought you would be close, you seem to be moving further and further apart. Ben's wife, Judith, wrote:

'We plunged into grief, desperate at times, angry, confused and lonely. Sometimes I felt a distance between my husband and myself. It hurt to see his pain and I couldn't help him. I was wounded too . . . Somehow, over the following weeks, we picked up the pieces. We had marvellous support. Best of all, we listened to each other and even though our reactions were sometimes very different – mine were violent and vocal, Ben tended to sink into a quiet depression – we managed to arrive at the same place, that of a sad but full acceptance of Richard's handicaps and death.'

Ben, writes of their struggle to help each other:

'Now was a time to share our real reactions. I told her, "As far as negative feelings are concerned, I reckon it's like clearing the weeds away from a flower bed. They need rooting out. If I don't face what I'm saying to myself I'll not be able to vent these feelings and clear them. Nothing positive will grow, and for Richard's sake, as well as our own, we've got to clear away the rubbish."

'In the days following Richard's death, Judith's feelings were vibrant and fluent. I believe I helped her express them. There was no point in either of us pretending that we didn't feel hurt or angry and I believe that unexpressed feelings grow deeply within oneself and are simply best aired, encountered, felt, owned and allowed to expend themselves. I had to listen as sensitively as I could, not just to the words, but to the music accompanying them. Sometimes she'd say things with which I didn't agree and we had to share our disagreement, knowing that unless we talked, cried and grieved together, we would inflict damage on ourselves.'

Sadly, not all couples are lucky enough, or have a strong enough relationship, to be able to help each other through to final acceptance of their loss. Some men become irritated at their partner's seeming lack of progress as the weeks go by; some may make the situation worse by telling their partners to start putting it behind them, to look to the future and to get on with life. If the woman is still crying after the first few weeks, or months, the man may think that there is something very wrong with her, a view which can be all too easily reinforced by others.

Whilst a woman may find it easy to open up to sympathetic listeners, there are few readily available outlets for a man to talk about his feelings of loss. Unless these differences are recognized and talked about, they can lead to immense stress in the relationship and in severe cases it can lead to the break-up of the mariage. If there have been problems before the bereavement, then the emotional strain of losing the baby can make such problems appear insurmountable.

Before matters reach this stage, it may be necessary for the couple to talk to someone who can assist with solving these disagreements. If the woman has to bottle up her emotions because she feels she cannot talk to her husband, this can affect their whole relationship. Whilst nothing can take away the pain itself, shared sorrow is easier to bear.

## OTHER MEMBERS OF THE FAMILY

There may be a need for other members of the family to see and hold the baby that has died. This may seem abhorrent to some people, yet it is quite acceptable for friends and family members to visit a Chapel of Rest to view an adult who has died. Unlike countries such as Australia and the North American continent where there is more awareness of the needs of other family members in this respect, in this country it is yet another taboo that surrounds the death of a baby. The matter does need sensitive handling, of course, but it can often be very important for some families to be involved in the bereavement.

## Siblings

In the film *Some Babies Die*, made in Australia, the events surrounding the stillbirth of a woman's fourth child are chronicled. The woman is allowed free access to her baby every day she is in hospital, following her Caesarian. Her children are encouraged to hold and touch the baby and to talk to him. It is a very moving film and one which should dispel some of the fears surrounding the involvement of children in the death of a baby. It is reassuring to see the matter-of-fact way the children accept that their little brother is dead. They are not in the least squeamish and they talk openly about their feelings, asking questions which are answered honestly and sensitively. Children are all too often kept out of the whole grieving process, with adults believing that it is important to shield them from something they will not understand. Yet, children can often accept death as something which is quite normal.

If a child is protected from all that surrounds a bereavement, it may make him or her very anxious and unable to ask vital questions. Children often believe, mistakenly, that it is something *they* have done which has led to the death of the baby. They may feel worried and afraid in case they, themselves, or their parents, suddenly die and disappear for ever. They need short and honest answers to their questions. Children are very demanding in normal situations, but they may be even more so in this one. It can be an immense strain if parents insist on giving less than honest answers.

Losing a baby can make parents over-protective of their other children. The children can seem so much more precious, which may lead to parents becoming over anxious about them. It is also common to imagine that a lost baby would have been perfect, that he or she would not have cried all the time or woken up at night or have had tantrums, and this can make parents impatient with the children they already have.

## Grandparents

It should be remembered, too, that grandparents were looking forward to the birth of their grandchild. Their grief is not just for the loss of the baby but for the pain and suffering that their own adult child is now going through. Most grandparents share the excitement of all the preparations for the forthcoming birth and they, too, think of that child's future. For them, as well, there is the upset of telling friends that their grandchild has died. Many grandparents feel utterly helpless, for they are unable to take away the pain of their own child, whilst at the same time perhaps feeling that it is wrong for them still to be in this world following the ending of such a precious new life.

It is quite normal for grandparents to go through all the various stages of grief and mourning in a similar way to the parents. However, it is important for them to be able to share their feelings with the parents, although for some this is difficult. If they have never been able to share their emotions before, then they may feel duty-bound to hide their feelings now, this being the best way of giving support as they see it. This may be interpreted, incorrectly, as a non-caring attitude which is made worse by the inability to mention the baby's name or even to acknowledge his or her existence. However, if grandparents can show their grief it can be a great comfort to parents to know that they care and understand.

Seeing the baby may help some grandparents to complete their own grieving; it is certainly an option that ought to be suggested to the parents; they may not think of it themselves, yet later wish they had done so. It can be a comfort to some families to be involved and an important part of the recovery process for them too.

## MEMORIES

Losing a baby is so intangible. Things happen so quickly that one can be in and out of hospital in a matter of hours. If those responsible for one's welfare do not help to provide memories, then it can seem as if nothing ever really happened and one may even question whether there was a baby at all.

### Seeing the Baby

When a baby is stillborn or miscarried late enough to be fully formed and big enough to be seen (and this can be as early as fourteen weeks), then it is important for the parents to have the opportunity of seeing and holding their child. Research has shown that it is a vital part of the grieving process. Indeed, it shows that the baby was a real person and can be remembered as such. Where this does not happen, everything can seem like a fantasy.

For some mothers, the need to see and hold their baby is a very natural feeling; it is the first thing they wish to do after the birth. For others, it may not be an easy decision to make, particularly if they have not been prepared. Some parents will need a little time to reach a decision and this is when sensitive counselling and reassurance by midwives and medical staff are so essential. If the parents refuse to see their baby, initially, they may subsequently regret such a decision, but are afraid to ask whether it is still possible a short while later. Initial refusal is often due to a mother's exhaustion, both mental and physical, or to the effect of pain-killing drugs administered during labour. It may be thought that it is too late for a change of mind or there may be a fear of seeing the baby at all; after all, it may be a first experience of seeing death. Those who refuse to see their baby may simply need support and encouragement to dispel some of their fears, and this can be done, for example, by describing the baby to them. If the parents are steadfast in their refusal, then a further approach could be made perhaps twenty-four hours later.

Of course, there may be a great fear of the unknown and many will be anxious about how the baby will look. Nevertheless, it is often the case that there is little to be afraid of and mothers frequently speak of their dead babies looking as if they were peacefully sleeping. By stressing this in a sensitive and gentle way and explaining why it is good to say hello and goodbye to their child, medical staff may give parents the courage to see their baby.

Many hospitals now provide Moses baskets to place miscarried and stillborn babies in, and this is an ideal way to introduce a baby to the more nervous. At first, they may just look at their baby wrapped up in the cradle. Then perhaps they might want to touch it; finally, they might wish to hold the little one in their arms. Very few women regret seeing their baby. Indeed, it is those who do not see their baby who most often express deep and lasting regret. They often say that they wish somebody had been there to help them in this respect. They may feel that they have rejected their baby and may try to visualize how it looked. This is when illogical feelings may be experienced such as imagining that their baby is alive in another part of the hospital.

It is comforting to note that parents rarely seem to notice the condition of the baby; they see only its beauty, not the defects that others may see. This altered perception should be taken into consideration by those who may feel obliged to make decisions on their behalf. For example, when a midwife looks at a stillborn baby, she will be seeing it as a professional and not with the eyes of a loving mother. Some professionals feel that it is their duty to shield parents from what they believe to be something unpleasant. Yet if they have the confidence to help the parents to see the child, whatever its condition, they are usually rewarded by the parents' reaction. As one parent said:

'I did not have the courage to see Katherine when she was

stillborn, the labour and the drugs had left me feeling out of control. Added to that, the reaction of the scan operator had left me with the belief that I had a monster inside me $Katherine was anencephallic – born without part of her cerebrum£. My husband saw her and he was shown her head, but all he could say was that she was beautiful with the most perfect lips he had ever seen. He said he was frightened to hold her, though, and has bitterly regretted that decision ever since.'

For those who produce an abnormal baby, this seeing and holding is even more important because the imagined horror is usually worse than reality. With careful wrapping, most babies can be seen and held. Seeing a perfect hand or foot or a beautiful face can provide a comforting memory. There is no need for a mother to see the handicap if she does not wish to. One mother whose baby was born with severe spina-bifida and other handicaps wrote:

'Elizabeth was beautiful. I was surprised. Her little hands and feet were perfect with fingers and toes complete. Her chest and head were perfect with wisps of red hair. I was surprised because I did not know what to expect; she was so much a baby. We kept her wrapped in her shawl while we stroked her face, arm and legs. We didn't look at her back, there was no need to. The midwife helped but she did not intrude.'

Only a few years ago, dead babies were spirited away immediately after delivery, in the belief that this would spare the parents unneccesary pain. It was believed that *not* seeing and holding the baby would make it easier to come to terms with the loss. However, it is not possible to put the birth and death of a baby out of one's mind by simply pretending that it has never happened. Those who have never seen their babies may never come to terms with their pain, and it remains locked away. As many as forty years later, such people speak of the sadness they feel because they were never allowed to acknowledge the existence of their baby or to openly grieve for it. Thankfully, it is now recognized that parents need to conceptualize their baby, to give it an identity, so that there is something to focus grief upon.

Of course, some parents will not be persuaded and will prefer not to see their child. This must be their choice. One mother who made this decision after her severely handicapped daughter was born said:

'I'm glad I didn't see Laura as she was in this world. I can look at my beautiful Amy and imagine Laura as she is now, whole and happy in God's arms.'

If a post-mortem examination has to be undertaken, it may still be possible to see the baby afterwards, if he or she is laid in a Moses cradle, carefully wrapped. Many hospitals do offer parents the chance to see the baby in the mortuary chapel and this can be an opportunity for them to bring in a special toy, some flowers, or simply to take their own photographs.

## Photographs

Even for those who see and hold their baby, memories soon fade. This is where a photograph of the baby is so important as a lasting reminder and proof of its existence. A photograph can provide a focus for parents to recognize and share their grief. Many hospitals now routinely take a Polaroid photo for the parents to take home, but these do not last for ever and should be rephotographed on to a good quality conventional film (this can be carried out by a local photographic studio). If parents do not wish to see or hold their baby, it is important that a photograph is taken and kept on file by the hospital. Such photographs can then be requested at a later date.

Some mothers worry about their need to keep looking at these photographs during the early days. Those around them may imply that it is somehow morbid. However, it is quite natural to want to look at them frequently at first, and this need does diminish with time. Gradually, photographs become comforting mementoes rather than painful reminders. Many parents want to put their treasured photographs on display, but they find that other people can be quite shocked by this, notwithstanding that a desire to display a picture of the child who meant so much is the most normal thing in the world.

## Dressing and Washing the Baby

Mothers frequently speak of the unfulfilled need they felt to dress their baby before it was buried or cremated, and this should have been made possible. Some mothers also express a desire to wash their child themselves, as an act of love and farewell. These wishes should be accommodated if at all possible. One mother wrote:

'Top of my list of regrets was that she should have been dressed in something pretty to be buried in, perhaps a christening gown, and that she should have had in her coffin the knitted toys that I had bought her. I definitely should have seen her and kissed her and said goodbye. I firmly believe that my emotional recovery would have been made easier if I had.'

Washing the baby themselves may be an important first step in the grieving process for the parents. Ben did just that for his baby son:

'I had decided that I wanted to wash Richard and wrap him up. He was so still. Although his little body was stiffening, I still felt a sensation of warmth in his head as I lifted him carefully from his cot. I could have washed him with my tears, they were plentiful enough. All I knew was that my gentle washing of him was an instinctive reaction, a gesture of care and potential love, already expressed in our common love for our first son, Edward. In that gesture were my fractured hopes; my deep-down longings. I cuddled him, sang to him and spoke some of the endearments I would have used had he been living. Something my mother said to me years before suddenly came back to me with compelling clarity. "It's not until you learn to let your children go that you really gain them." As I cried I became aware that Judith and Ellen had joined me. We held him together for the last time and I placed him gently back in his cot and kissed him goodbye.'

## Memory Book

Many parents compile a memory book, or a memory box, into which go all the photographs, letters from friends and family, cards and ribbons from flowers, the copy of the birth certificate or the copy of the Certificate of Registration of Stillbirth, maybe a print-out from a heart monitor or a photograph of a scan. These can be shared with future children and will help to keep alive the memories.

Some hospitals provide other mementoes of the baby, such as a lock of hair, a name band, or a cot tag. In America, they often provide hand and footprints, details of weight, length, head circumference, time of birth, the midwife or doctor's name and the name of the ward. It is always worth asking for these things.

## Book of Remembrance

Many people give their lost babies a name and some hospitals now provide a special Babies' Book of Remembrance, in which the baby's name and a simple inscription can be inserted. This is a great comfort, particularly to those who have miscarried and have so few tangible memories and no grave to visit.

## Service of Remembrance

In many parts of the country, various self-help groups, together with hospital chaplains, come together once a year for special services, at which all the babies lost during pregnancy or at birth can be remembered. They are very moving occasions. As one person wrote:

'This service provides an opportunity for sharing memories and sadness. With so many people gathered together and having shared such traumatic and sad experiences, I had expected it to be a harrowing occasion, but it proved to be deeply moving yet full of hope and joy. The service booklet front cover was colourfully illustrated with flowers, the hymns were well-chosen and the readings and poems highlighted in a sensitive manner some anguishing feelings about miscarriage, stillbirth, neo-natal death and the pain of loss.

'Half-way through the service the names of lost babies were read out and then we lit our candles, one for each tiny life, and placed them in the stand. I found this a deeply moving experience ... The prayers and readings which followed made a great impact and I'm sure that I was not alone in feeling an overwhelming healing calmness descending at that time.'

It does need someone to suggest these things, as many parents do not know what is possible or 'permissible'. They may be too afraid to make their own requests known and so the opportunity passes.

## Post-Mortem

It is usual to ask for permission to perform a post-mortem examination of a baby, in order to try to determine the cause of death. Parents needs to be approached with sensitivity at this time as some may feel, understandably, that it is a violation of their child's body. Most parents, however, are anxious to find out all they can about their baby's death and will agree to an autopsy.

If an autopsy does reveal the cause of death, it may help doctors to find ways of preventing or treating the problem in a future pregnancy. Parents may be offered the chance of genetic counselling if their baby was found to be abnormal, so that they may know what the chances are of a recurring problem in the future.

## BURIAL ARRANGEMENTS

An important part of the grieving process is the need to say a final farewell to the baby, and parents are now encouraged to attend either a burial or a cremation. Indeed, more and more parents of miscarried babies are demanding that their baby receive a dignified ending.

By law, a baby that is stillborn after twenty-eight weeks' gestation must be buried or cremated. Many hospitals still make all the arrangements for the burial or cremation of the baby and this may be organized very quickly after the birth. Parents may be asked to make important decisions about their baby's final resting place at a time when they are emotionally unfit to make such a decision. As a consequence, it is often the case that the couple agrees to the hospital handling all the arrangements. Because of their distress, however, they may even miss attending the burial or cremation. Unquestionably, hospital staff act with the best of motives, but in attempting to relieve parents of any more distress, as they see it, they may end up denying the parents an important aspect of the grieving and healing process.

Parents should have all the options placed before them, and should be allowed time to make up their minds. The starkest action on the part of a hospital is for a baby to be stillborn one day, for example, have a post-mortem the next, and to be buried a day later. Such haste is unjustifiable and may cause a considerable amount of distress later to grieving parents.

Several options are available, yet many parents remain unaware of them. A baby may be buried or cremated by the hospital, often with the hospital chaplain officiating, with the parents attending if they so wish. If this method is chosen, a baby may be buried in a mass grave, occupied by up to twelve or more babies. Such graves are usually unmarked and no headstone is allowed to be erected. This can be a cause of distress, later, when parents realize that their baby's name will not be appearing on the grave. Also, it may take many months for the grave to be completed, so, until it is finished, there may be nowhere to leave flowers. An unkempt heap will be the only evidence of the baby's presence.

An example of good practice is that offered by St Mary's Maternity Hospital, in Portsmouth. Here, parents are offered the chance of burial or cremation, which is arranged by the hospital. The chaplain takes an active part in the service and parents, of course, can attend. Parents can choose to have their tiny loved ones buried in a small plot for six babies, with a headstone. The headstone is paid for in equal shares and all the babies' names appear. Parents may also choose a similar, unmarked grave. Many hospitals are now changing their policies as a result of pressure from parents and support groups such as SANDS (Stillbirth and Neonatal Death Society). Their address appears on page 210.

Parents can, of course, opt for a private funeral. Single plots in certain cemeteries are free and this can be established, locally. A baby may also be buried in a churchyard. In both cases, a headstone can be purchased and erected.

Although there is no legal requirement to bury a baby of less than twenty-eight weeks' gestation, parents do have the legal right to do so and many are now asking for this to happen. However, certain hospitals appear not to realize that this is a legal right and still continue their disposal techniques via the hospital waste disposal system.

Some hospitals do offer parents a dignified ending to their baby's life. For example, Portsmouth cremates all miscarried babies of approximately fourteen weeks' gestation and over, and the hospital chaplain holds a special service.

If parents wish to have their miscarried baby buried, all that is required is a written authority to give to the funeral directors to allow for the burial. This could take the form of a letter from the doctor who attended the mother, giving brief details of the circumstances, certifying that the baby was of less than twenty-eight weeks' gestation, and that no registrar's certificate for burial is required by law.

It can be a great comfort to parents to organize the funeral themselves, choosing hymns and readings and whatever else they may think is appropriate. It may be necessary, however, to approach several funeral directors before a sympathetic one is found. Ben and Judith did just that; Ben wrote:

'Two things were important to me. The first was to support Judith as best I could. The second was to arrange a fitting conclusion to Richard's short life and here I had what I can only call instinctive reactions that needed to be met. I managed to find a firm of funeral directors who would faithfully cater for our needs and I explained that, apart from collecting Richard's body and putting him into a casket and keeping him until we were ready to say our farewells, I wanted them to maintain a background position. I wanted to collect his casket and carry it into the chapel myself where we would hold a short service. Judith and I would then take him to the crematorium in our car and take him inside the building ourselves. I knew this was not customary, but I also knew that I didn't want our grieving to be removed from us by the respectful professional ministrations of others.

'We held a short service, which, with the help of a friend who was a priest, we constructed together. We chose music that reflected our own selves and hopes. We held a communion service with bread we had baked ourselves, together with our favourite wine. These we shared with a small group of friends gathered around Richard's diminutive white casket, on which stood a small arrangement of flowers from our garden. As a final gesture, Judith and I carried the casket into the crematorium together, placing it on the dais, kissing it and leaving in tears.'

Of course, not everyone would wish to do this, and here a suportive hospital chaplain or parish priest is often the best person to approach. The main thing is that parents should be given *time*. If they feel hurried into making decisions at a time of complete shock, they may, later, have deep and lasting regrets about how their baby's ending was dealt with.

## GOING HOME

Returning home after the loss of a baby is often very difficult. In many instances the mother's initial reaction after the loss of her baby is to want to run away, to escape from the hospital environment that has brought her so much unhappiness. Those who for medical reasons have to stay in hospital for longer, may find that they are haunted by the cries of other babies in nurseries near to the post-natal wards. They may wish to remain in their room, away from others, not knowing how to cope with mothers who have just given birth to healthy babies. They may feel embarrassed at having to tell others what has happened to their baby. Well-intentioned staff may try to encourage them to join the others for meals, but unless the woman specifically requests this, it is probably kinder to let her take her meals in her own room.

It may be the case that after several days in hospital it is hard to leave, for there is an element of being cocooned from the real world. Once the hospital is left, reality has to be faced. One woman who miscarried recalls:

'All the time I was in hospital it was as if it was happening to someone else. I didn't care what they did to me. I just went along with it. It was only when my husband came to collect me and I stepped out of the door that it hit me that I had lost my baby and that I was walking out as an empty shell.'

When a baby is stillborn or dies soon after birth, the house may be fully prepared for the return of a new baby. The nursery may be ready and new items left lying unpacked. It can be difficult for the man to know what to do for the best. Should he pack everything away before his partner returns home, or should he leave it for her to do? Will the sight of a baby's apparel cause more pain for her? This is a difficult question to answer and ought to be discussed with the woman herself. Well-intentioned friends may consider that it is best if the house is cleared of all such reminders. However, it can be an important part of the grieving process to pack such things away for oneself. It may be distressing; it may cause tears, but this can be of more help than finding everything hastily bundled into the attic, for example, after so much care and anticipation has gone into preparing the room. Trying to deny the baby's existence by removing all the evidence may not be in the best interests of a grieving woman.

# THE HELP OF OTHERS

Other people's negative reactions have already been discussed in an earlier part of the book, and are very similar in all bereavement tragedies. Positive reactions have also been discussed, but it is important to make a special mention here about support groups for those suffering the loss of a baby. As time passes you may feel that you cannot keep telling friends and family about your feelings, that their interest will wane and that they will become bored. A support group, on the other hand, can offer comfort for as long as it is needed. Such groups usually hold regular meetings where parents can meet and talk with other bereaved parents. One member said:

'At the time, I felt that the support I was getting from my family and friends was adequate. As time went by, many of them spoke about Simon less and less, including my husband. After all, he was back at work having to fulfil his responsibilities there once again, and so seemed to slip back into a routine. After two or three months I was being told by some people to "Pull up your socks; life has to go on; it's been long enough now to put it all behind you and to stop being so miserable."

'What they couldn't see was that the more this was said, the more despair I felt. I still felt the need to talk about him, not only about my grief, but also in a way that many mothers talk about their babies – how much hair he had, who he looked like, etc. – and to share my photos, show him off, so to speak (no one wanted to look at photos of a baby who had died; I think, somehow, they thought it was eerie).

'At my first meeting, it was so nice to be told that it hadn't been very long at all, that I was still in the early days and that I had every right to be upset. I was able to show people my photos and it was nice to be told that he was a lovely baby. At last I had found some people who understood the despair, and I could talk about Simon and the way I felt for as long as I liked, without feeling uneasy or as though he was a taboo subject. Also, it was helpful to read about other people's feelings and to

135

know that we weren't the only ones. Before joining the group, I felt a bit of an outcast. After the first few meetings, I would go home and cry buckets, although I must say I felt a lot better for it. Also, I would stay awake until the early hours of the morning reading everything I had been given that evening. It acted like a real tonic. The group was so inspiring that I felt compelled to write down my story. Hopefully, I have helped others. Where else would I have been encouraged to do so?'

Some people, though, are reluctant to turn to others for help, as though asking for help were a sign of weakness or failure to cope alone. It is, however, a very positive step, in that one recognizes that one has gone as far as one can on one's own. There is enormous relief to be found in talking to people who understand how one is feeling because they have been there themselves. It is surprising just how quickly a self-help group can encourage an improvement in one's state of mind. It will be realized that loneliness is not inevitable; that others have similarly suffered; that the wide range of emotions experienced are not abnormal; and that others have lost a baby and survived and have often had a healthy baby a while later.

This can help to restore confidence in oneself and one's ability to have a child. It is a great help, too, to know that there are always others to talk to, no matter what the circumstances.

## THE NEXT TIME

Losing a baby rarely diminishes the intense longing for another child. Bereavement is usually followed by the desire to fill the gap that has been left in one's life, despite the fear of a similar tragedy happening again.

However, everyone is different. Some will wish to wait whilst others will not. For those who feel they cannot wait too long to have another child, it *is* advisable to have a period of mourning before undertaking what may become a very harrowing pregnancy. Ultimately, of course, this must be a personal decision unless there are medical reasons for imposing a delay. It is by no means unusual for those who do conceive again very quickly to find a coincidence in the timing, which, needless to say, can be very distressing as well as confusing.

A too-rapid conception may also lead the mother to put her emotions on ice for the period of her pregnancy; consequently, she may find that, upon the birth of the next baby, all her grief and sorrow return to her. Feeling that one has come to terms with one's loss only to find that this is not the case after all, can be a tremendous shock. Indeed, some women have concentrated for so long on their pregnancy and the process of having a baby, that actually producing a live child can be extremely traumatic for them. Some try to convince themselves, whilst carrying the child, that there is no baby, in the hope that should a tragedy recur, they will at least have protected themselves from more pain and grief:

'I tried to forget that I was pregnant. I decided that I wouldn't go to any ante-natal classes, or get anything ready for the baby. It was almost as if I thought putting the new baby to the back of my mind would ensure that he would be all right in the end, and that I would not be hurt again.'

Support during a subsequent pregnancy is very important. It is a time fraught with anxieties; every twinge can lead to panic in the mother-to-be. This is when an understanding GP, consultant, midwife or health visitor can be of much help. So, too, can the support of self-help groups. Positive support may also be given at ante-natal classes where the parents will meet up with others whose expectations are not clouded by previous tragedies:

'About half-way through the pregnancy my outlook changed. I could not consider the new baby to be responsible for the tragedy that had befallen us and I had to consider his well-being. We looked at the worst scenario, put it to one side and just hoped. I couldn't alter the fact that we had lost a baby, but I could look on this new life in a positive way.

I went back to ante-natal classes. It felt good to be positive and to be with people whose outlook was optimistic. I felt "normal" about my pregnancy.'

Of course, it would not be normal to have no worries and fears. Many women find pregnancy an anxious time, especially the days leading up to the birth, when all their hopes are pinned on a happy outcome:

'At some time during the last three weeks of pregnancy, this optimistic atmosphere disappeared without trace. I imagined everything going wrong. My nerves were very taut. I cried a lot. I became frantic. My husband found it hard to keep me calm. Afterwards he told me that as I panicked, he could feel himself panicking also, yet he managed to hold on to his true feelings. It must have been difficult for him not to catch my fears.'

Once the baby is born there may be a sense of elation at finally having made it. There may be a great sense of healing:

'When Joseph was delivered, he was silent. Then there seemed to be a pause and then he cried. That sound was the most overwhelming thing that has happened to me. I was totally struck with emotion. I sobbed with tears of sheer happiness and total relief; it was the most moving experience of my life.

'The thought of Daniel, who was stillborn, brings tears to my eyes and hurts me inside. This feeling will, I'm sure, always remain with me, but it is greatly eased with the birth of Joseph. Joseph will never replace that poor, limp body that we lost, but it is a joy to have him and a good feeling knowing that twenty-three months – yes, twenty-three months – of pregnancy have not been wasted.'

For a few unlucky mothers, the days following the birth of a healthy baby can be filled with confusion. It may be a time of celebration and joy for the new life, yet intense sadness for the baby who is not there. There may be a period of depression,

138

and this can be difficult for others to understand – after all, one has spent months anxiously awaiting this baby and here it is, apparently healthy, yet the mother is depressed. Simon's mother vividly describes her feelings:

'When we arrived home it was such a relief, but my mind kept flashing back to the time when I came home before; when I started packing all the baby clothes and other things away as soon as we had walked in the door.

'For the first few weeks things were fine, but then my husband went back to work and I found myself thinking about Simon a lot. It was difficult to understand why I was so upset, now that I had everything I wanted. I suppose it was because although I had Ben, I still wanted Simon. Although I was over the moon with Ben, I don't think I appeared bubbly enough for my visitors. But how could I tell them why? By the time Ben was six weeks old I was beginning to feel better, and now at ten weeks I'm beginning to feel guilty at feeling better; and looking back, I think I probably missed out on Ben by being preoccupied with Simon.

'I've just crossed another hurdle this week. A couple we know have just had a baby and they have called him Simon. It just goes to show; there will always be situations to cope with.'

If these feelings of confusion and grief continue, then help should be sought. There may be a very real possibility of post-natal depression. It should be remembered that the weeks following the birth are just as taxing for a woman who has previously lost a baby as they are for any new parent; unfortunately, it may be more difficult for a previously bereaved mother to express her tiredness and frustrations for fear of others considering her to be ungrateful.'

## IN CONCLUSION

Parents frequently ask the question: 'How long will it take us to get over the loss of our baby?' Of course, there can be no definitive answer. It may be that getting over it never really happens. As one parent wrote, ten years after her son died within twenty-four hours of his birth:

'Getting over it implies that you no longer think about your loss; you no longer want or need to talk about it; that something has happened to make you forget or has put things right. All of us in the group know that none of this can ever be true. What a pity most friends, relatives and dare I say it, husbands, don't seem to understand this.

'Nothing can turn the clock back and return to us the child that we have lost. A new baby can never replace the lost one, which is something others find difficult to understand. But, gradually, over the months and years, you come to terms with your loss. You accept it as something that happened in the past and which, although it shapes how you think, feel and react, no longer dominates or haunts your every minute of the day. Slowly you come to realize that other thoughts and ideas *can* occupy your mind; that plans for the future *can* be made and carried out. Slowly, very slowly, the pain and grieving ease and life can begin to be lived again.'

## To Those Who Mourn Their Children

Do not weep because you think you have forever lost the fairest flower in your garden. The truth is that the flower has been transplanted into a far more beauteous garden where it sheds a greater perfume and is lovelier and more beautiful than ever it could be on earth. It has been spared many of Earth's sadnesses and sorrows. It has been spared many cruelties and many blights. Your child will never know much that has darkened your own life. Rejoice that freedom has come to a young soul who will never be distressed by the many miseries that afflict your world. Do not grieve for the child; grieve if you will for your own loss, for you will miss the little radiant face, the childish prattle, the diminutive figure. But, though your physical eyes cannot see, and your physical ears cannot hear, your child is ever present. If you stop shedding tears that create a mist in front of your eyes, you will see the truth that in God's great Kingdom, there is no death and all continue to live in far better conditions in a world which is richer and sweeter than anything you have ever dreamed. Do not sorrow for the child. Know that an all-loving God has given angels to protect her or him and the child will, in fullness of time, be reunited with you.

*Silver Birch, an Indian spirit sage*

# 9  The Death of a Parent

The invisible barrier between ourselves and our own earthly destiny is stripped away when we are faced with the deaths of those who have protected and loved us, who have inspired and guided us, who may have dominated and suppressed us: in other words, our parents. Their deaths remind us profoundly of our own mortality, and of the fact that we are now the older generation. Parents are always there as we grow up. They seem a permanent fixture – perhaps even an irritating one at times – and very little consideration is given to the prospect of their dying. As we reach adulthood ourselves, the death of our parents may cross our minds uneasily from time to time, but any thought of suffering is usually hastily brushed aside.

## FRIENDS OR STRANGERS

Parental attitudes toward their children are often conditioned by the role they assume and the image and expectations they have of themselves as guide and example. Consequently a child may have great difficulty getting to know its parents as *people*, and the problem can continue well into later life: it is not necessarily confined to the formative years. A parent's need to maintain constant supremacy by always knowing what is best for the child is unnecessary and prevents the parent/child relationship – a sometimes less than loving one – from developing into one more resembling friendship, which has its own closeness of feeling.

People are generally expected to grieve profoundly for a dead parent. When this seems not to be the case, the type of relationship they shared ought perhaps to be looked at. Here a man of forty-three recounts his experience:

'I felt sad when my father died, after all, he was my flesh and blood. But when I tried to analyse exactly what I was feeling I couldn't really find an answer. It was more sadness for him than for me, I felt. He had always been so high-handed; everything that a child and a teenager enjoys when they are growing up was frowned upon. Sometimes, I suspected that he liked some of the music of the sixties, but because it was "teenage" music it *had* to be condemned and even banned. I had to get permission to do everything and I was always being reminded that I was living under *his* roof and that I could be asked to leave at any time. One day I called his bluff and moved into a flat with friends. The reduced space was worth all the compromises; at least I was with people who had similar interests and knew the meaning of the word tolerance. The old man tried to get me back home but I refused. I was hoping he would lose his holier-than-thou attitude after I had left, but I was wrong. It went on and on right up to the day he died. The thing which really got my goat was that he was never like it with his grandchildren. They were the apple of his eye and became almost playmates. I was always the child, though.

Loved him? Well, I suppose I did, but I just couldn't bring myself to cry for someone whom I was supposed to have loved. In fact, I tried to induce it several times, just for appearances, without very much success. After all, that's what's expected isn't it?'

The problem here was the mutual inflexibility of father and son in their attitudes towards each other. It was obviously too late for the father to change; if the son had been flexible enough to accept his father as he was, instead of wishing he was something else, he might have had a proper opportunity to grieve. If he had tried to be more understanding of his father's point of view – admittedly less than reasonable – they might have been brought closer during the last years of his father's life, and might well have become friends at last.

However, it may be the case that a relationship does not need such compromises. Here is a forty-five year old man talking about his mother, aged sixty-seven:

143

'My mother was a great loss. I felt almost embarrassed, even in front of my wife, at the feelings I had of such desolation when she died. I have to say from the outset, though, that it was not the loss of a parent I had experienced. It was the loss of someone who had become one of my greatest friends. Sure, growing up had been a bit of a pain, at times, with the parental bit making itself felt, as a result of which I had complained loudly from time to time. But looking back, I can trace the seeds of our friendship from about my early teens.

It really started to grow from my late teens onwards, following on from the "awkward" teenage period. I'm surprised really that it didn't arrive sooner, as getting me to do anything was always easier if a low-key approach was adopted and the heavy-handed parental bit was dropped. My mother and I shared the most idiotic sense of humour. We would burst out laughing at things of which only we could see the funny side. My father would often be completely puzzled, but usually joined in when he saw us in such fits.

Our relationship became so easy and smooth. She would often say, "I'm supposed to be your mother", to which I would reply in imitation of John McEnroe, "*You cannot be serious!*" Whenever the parental part of her emerged I would just tease it out of her by pretending to sulk. Immediately she went into reverse and approached me as her friend. Words cannot describe just how different her two hats were. One made me feel cold and uncomfortable – even rebellious – even in later years. The other made me feel really good and that I was in the presence of someone I loved and respected very much. To have had a parent whom I freely chose as one of my best friends is indescribable.'

## STILL WANTING TO TELL

The childish wish to run to our parents and tell them our news never really leaves any of us. No matter how old we become, we long to share our successes with our parents and make them proud of us. Unless we are comforted by the thought that they are still watching over us from wherever they are now, it can be very sad to think that they knew us only up to a certain point in our lives, before we realized our potential and matured into the kind of people we are today.

However, although we may feel that we have changed, it is unlikely that they would be of the same opinion; loving parents will have been aware of our capabilities long before we were, and though, of course, they would be delighted by our achievements, they probably would not have been surprised.

We may also continue to turn to a parent for advice at times of crisis. One woman described how she had to keep reminding herself not to go rushing along to the next street to knock on her parents' front door whenever she needed help. Her mother had been a source of great comfort to her during her early married life, and the fact that she had died sixteen years ago and that the house had been sold shortly afterwards, had not altered the woman's impulse to seek solace in her mother's arms in times of trouble.

## STILL WANTING TO KNOW

The death of a parent can raise questions which will never be answered. Did the parent realize how much he or she was loved? Did the bereaved adult appear to be taking the parent for granted? Perhaps it may be felt that opportunities to express love and appreciation were wasted.

Important issues that were never discussed because the time wasn't right may now become of great concern.

'My mother told me at a very early age that it might have been possible for me to have had a small brother or sister, if things had been different. I was an only child and was quite used to being an only child. In fact, I didn't particularly want a little brother or sister and couldn't imagine what sort of different situation she was referring to. I never pursued the question but what she told me never left my mind. Odd references to the subject were occasionally made as I grew up and I was always told that I would understand as I got older. The idea of there being a problem during my mother's pregnancy was slowly realized, however. But mention of the subject gradually disappeared altogether.

The fact that my mother must have had a miscarriage or something even worse, now makes me want to hear from her just what happened to her and that little being who was a part of me and my family. Could I have consoled her or made the deprivation she must have felt any easier to bear? I long to be able to talk to her about it, but now I shall never know; and all because of unnecessary feelings of embarrassment or whatever it may have been.'

'Whilst going through Dad's things, I came across some important bits and pieces from his place of work. Others might have thought he had misappropriated them. I know he couldn't possibly have done. There must be a very good reason for them being there, but only Dad could tell us what the reason is. I couldn't possibly have handed them back, how could I have done? To have caused the good memory of my father to become tarnished in the minds of others would have been almost a betrayal. If only he was here to provide what must have been a straightforward explanation.'

'I don't think either of my parents really understood me. I always felt a disappointment to them because their expectations of me were never the same as my own. It was never discussed, though. It now seems so sad for them to have gone through life thinking in this way. We should have put all our cards on the table and had a frank discussion when the opportunity was there. I'm sure our respective positions would have been clarified, leading to a much better understanding between us. The chance to do what should have been done during their lifetime has now been wasted.'

A dying parent may want to make a last-minute revelation. This may be a need to clear a troubled conscience, or to share regrets about a wasted life or missed opportunities; or perhaps to express remorse for being an inadequate spouse or parent. It may be felt there is the possibility of leaving behind some of their unhappiness with their loved ones, who will somehow begin to atone for them. The bereaved adult will then be left to complete the cycle in the sense of trying to understand and to forgive, both for his or her own sake and for the sake of the parent.

## ASSUMING THE ROLE OF PARENT TO A PARENT

Parenting a parent during the last phase of his or her life is often a non-decision; whilst it is a situation that may not have been freely entered into, neither is it one into which people are coerced. Assuming responsibility for the quality of life of a dying parent has its roots in a lifetime's relationship.

'The thought of Daddy going into a home with lots of people he did not know, because he had had his first stroke, was too horrible to contemplate. It would be like sending him to prison for something he hadn't done. If I'd listened to my husband and my brother he would have ended up away from his family. He needed us more than ever, then. I had to insist that I would take responsibility for him at home.'

Looking after a terminally ill parent may give rise to upset feelings in retrospect. The carer may feel that too strict an approach was adopted, even though it seemed at the time to be for the parent's 'own good'; afterwards it may seem that perhaps the parent's wishes were not taken into sufficient account, and possibly this was a cause of unnecessary distress.

'Mum started to have these recurring phases which made her very stubborn. Once she had made up her mind that she wanted something done or wanted to go somewhere, nothing would stop her from trying to get her own way. Most of her demands were quite unrealistic. At times, I felt myself

147

beginning to lose patience even though I knew she couldn't help it. On more than one occasion I threatened her with an ultimatum, that if she didn't stop it I would send her away, permanently. She would then go quiet and wouldn't talk for hours. It gave me some needed relief. Looking back, though, I often cry myself to sleep thinking how I scolded my own mother. It's the last thing I wanted to do, and the thought of my causing my own mother to be so very unhappy during these phases upsets me dreadfully.'

'He had lung cancer and not long to live. I tried to prevent him from smoking, as if this could have improved his condition. Why didn't I see that stopping the damage was too late? Cigarettes were a real source of pleasure, perhaps the only pleasure he had left; and I tried to deny him that pleasure.'

Being caregiver to a parent reverses everything we have come to assume throughout our lives. It is taken for granted that a parent's duty is to tend to a child's needs; it is not a child's duty – even an adult child – to tend to the intimate needs of a parent. There may be feelings of distress, even of shame, on the part of a parent because everyday activities can no longer be performed without assistance from caregiving offspring.

Any need to maintain an outward sense of dignity, however, can easily conflict with such practical considerations as maintaining personal hygiene, giving rise to reactions that may be perceived as awkwardness, but which are more likely to be attempts to assert independence. Achieving a new kind of independence through the care of an adult child is not believed possible. Similarly, the carer may not understand this need of the parent to make a bid for independence: 'I know he couldn't help it, but he was so cussed. I understand why, now. I just wish I could have understood at the time.'

The decisions taken whilst caring for a dying parent may be reviewed time and time again, with endless agonizing over whether they were the right ones:

'We managed for a time at home. Things went as well as they

could have done. Then the decision to send her to a hospice was taken. It was taken only because coping had become very difficult. What I only found out some six months after she had died was that she could have stayed at home for much longer. Proper additional care could have been brought into the home which would have been enough to keep us together. I just wasn't told, though – no one had ever told me that such a thing was possible, not even my own doctor, and I was stupid enough not to have found out for myself.'

Wanting to feel that the best possible care was given to a dying parent can give rise to such feelings. There may even be self-torment for having taken on the caring role at all because it is felt the pressures were too great for the carer to be able to provide optimum care.

It may also be felt that insufficient time was allocated to the role of caring, in that it was only one of many commitments; consequently, there may be a feeling of relief when such an enormous pressure is lifted, and this, ironically, may also lead to feelings of guilt. Such ambivalent emotions will need to be released with the help of supportive and sympathetic listeners. Other aspects of caring for a loved one at home are considered in Chapter 4 in 'The Emotional Side of Caring at Home', page 46.

## THE LOSS OF A PARENT

No matter how prepared we may feel, the death of a parent is likely to be profoundly distressing. Behaving in an 'adult' manner may be thought possible in advance of the event, but losing a mother or father, in whatever circumstances, will give rise to unpredictable feelings. The attitude that it is immature for an adult child to display feelings of grief at the death of a parent stems from society's expectations of us to maintain a stiff upper lip.

'All my life I tried to convince myself that I was independent and that I could easily survive without my parents. Privately, I always thought it was a bit cissyish to have feelings of missing my mother and father, especially when I was away on business trips abroad. Perhaps I tried to over-compensate by suppressing such feelings ... When I lost my father, my age was irrelevant. I just kept thinking of all the lovely times we had together as I grew up. The Hornby trainset with the tank locomotive, the walks, the kite-flying and the records we used to play together... I just wept and kept thinking, "My dad's died".'

Men in particular are expected to keep control of themselves. Expressions of grief, especially unexpected ones, may be thought extraordinary by others. It may be the case that a spouse is less than supportive, or simply fails to understand how the partner is feeling at such a time. Such a lack of emotional care can easily compound feelings of grief; empathetic support must be sought outside the family where such a situation exists, in order to come to terms with the loss:

'I felt more comfortable talking away from the family. They were all going through a difficult time and I felt I just had to get away and open up my feelings to someone who wasn't going to clam up at certain things I needed to say. I was able to learn about the reality of my loss and exactly what I was feeling. I talked about what dad and I meant to each other and how we probably saw each other ...

I was able to talk about the things I wished dad and I could have done together and the things I now miss so much. I was really able to let out the very intense feelings that I had, such as my sense of deprivation, sadness and anger at the way he had to die. This gave me the opportunity to begin learning about why I felt the way I did. *Having* to seek outside help turned out to be good for me.'

The bereaved may feel a need for solitude and wish to get completely away from other people. A country churchyard can often provide the ideal environment.

Writing too, can be a great comfort, particularly when it is difficult to talk. It provides the opportunity to go over those feelings that were experienced at the time and to get a better understanding of them, and of what is felt now. Finding new angles by reading and re-reading what one has written can also bring about a better understanding of the situation.

The question of whether any of a parent's belongings should be kept as a permanent memento is a very personal one. Some unintentionally cruel decisions can be imposed by those who are in a position to exercise authority; for instance, the husband and father who insisted on clearing out everything belonging to his wife as soon as possible after her death, thus causing a great deal of distress to other family members. On the other hand, relatives and friends may hint that hanging on to things is rather unhealthy, with the result that keeping personal items becomes secretive, almost something to be ashamed of:

'I keep my father's hat, coat and gloves in an old chest with lots of things on top. My husband knows they're there and doesn't mind at all. He knows they're important to me, but we never talk about it. I mentioned it to a colleague at work, once. I learned quickly. I've never mentioned it since.'

Disapproval on the part of others in this respect may be a peculiarity of these islands. In Mediterranean countries, for instance, the passing down of treasured items of clothing from generation to generation is considered quite normal. Wearing them, too, especially on festive occasions, is also the norm. Why should such horror and disgust be expressed in this country, therefore, at the prospect of someone wishing to store in a safe place just a little of that which belonged to a parent? Keeping such personal items can be a comforting reminder of them, and is quite different to turning a room or even a house into a shrine. Such a sad situation would need the help of specialist counselling.

Over a period of time, as the healing takes place, those personal items which may have seemed so very important at first will become less symbolic, and it will probably be felt that some at least can now be parted with. However the need to keep some special memento of those we held so dear is unlikely to disappear altogether.

# 10 Towards the Future

Life presents us with a series of bereavements. As children, we may feel bereaved at suddenly being deprived of our parents for a short while when they are away from us, for example. It is usually our first experience of a kind of bereavement. Upsets and disappointments continue to pervade our lives, creating further kinds of bereavement; but we somehow survive them; we carry on. We learn that it is possible to overcome such upsets and that they are a part of living.

Our first experience of a loved one's death is our first experience of a major bereavement. No two people are likely to have exactly the same feelings, and the experience of emerging from grief will be unique for each one of us. We will feel our own pain in our own way and it will last for a time that is appropriate for each of us. Time alone will not heal; this can only be achieved by the imperceptible building of bridges across the chasm of grief, enabling a slow healing to take place.

Travelling the road of grief and emerging intact will mean a slow transition. It will involve replacing a longing for a lost 'me' that was part of a special relationship, and allowing a new 'me' to emerge. A 'me' that will no longer ache so much for the past to be returned, but sees the past as being a period of privilege, the ending of which is not the end of life itself, but the start of a future with new opportunities which ought not to be allowed to slip from our grasp.

The healing of grief cannot be measured in the same terms as a physical wound; its course is uneven and unpredictable. We may feel we have reached a certain point in our progress only to find ourselves seemingly sliding backwards. This is not a cause for alarm; it is simply part of the journey, one individual's way of dealing with all the adjustments necessary in order to proceed further. Fluctuating moods of sadness, anger and anxiety, for example, are an indication that the journey is underway, and such emotions will gradually become mixed with more peaceful feelings.

## AVOIDING REPENTING AT LEISURE

The period following a death is a time to avoid major decision-making. True feelings and wishes cannot surface; the desperate decisions of today may become the regrets of tomorrow. There may be a sudden inclination to move house as soon as possible, or to start selling those things that so profoundly remind one of the person who has died. Much upset can be caused later as a result of such actions. It is far better to sit tight and realize that major decisions can only properly be made in the light of a new beginning. Grief cannot be disposed of by getting rid of those things that remind us of our heartache; they are best put to one side until a more objective view is possible.

Unless there are unavoidable financial circumstances, it is much better not to move home as a kind of reflex action, even though those closest may suggest that this is for the best. Regardless of one's surroundings, life without the lost loved one will have to be faced. Those of advancing years who have succumbed to the temptation to forge a new life in a new house, or in the homes of sons or daughters, often express profound regrets later at such hasty decision-making. Trying to reverse such a decision will be difficult, at best. Realizing the need to accept a new independence, however, is often a key factor in a healthy emotional and physical adjustment. Sole independence is not the same as isolation; it means having control over one's own life, being able to make decisions by oneself, for oneself. Getting used to this new independence may be easier in familiar surroundings; certainly it is easier to reciprocate gestures of friendship made by others if one is in one's own home.

# READJUSTMENT

The passing milestones on the road to healing will be recognized. Facing the routine tasks of living and accepting responsibilities will seem less burdensome. The ability to make decisions returns, with the confidence that *right* decisions can be taken, whether on important or trivial matters.

Sounds and smells often remind us of places and activities, pinpointing times past; such reminders will become less painful and will emerge as peaceful symbols of that which has been cherished.

Completing the journey of grief will mean 'unlearning' much of what has been learned from being part of a team. Individual needs and life-style have been modified and adapted to a partnership with the lost loved one, and now all that experience has no focus – it is suddenly redundant. New ways will have to be learnt to deal with a completely new scenario.

It is possible that some who are undergoing the journey of grief have discovered for the first time a very positive side to family members. Fearing that this new-found closeness may be only temporary, they might be tempted to extend the true period of grief artificially in order to prolong their enjoyment of such newly-discovered relationships. However, they will have to realize that a time will come when the relationship needs to develop honestly and that allowing the situation to drift along on false pretences can only bring about what they most fear.

## New Goals

The loss of a loved one can mean an opportunity to discover talents that have never been used before or to realize unfulfilled ambitions. It is an opportunity to put self first and to achieve new personal goals. This cannot be classed as being selfish or an insult to the memory of the lost loved one. Foregoing any such ambitions during his or her life was the definitive act of unselfishness. Life has now changed, and one could be said to have a duty to go forward in a constructive and meaningful way. Additionally, carrying on an interest, even a business that was so much a part of a lost loved one's life, may provide much comfort.

Of course, achieving new goals will take time and patience. Setting small attainment targets each day is probably the best way of starting. It is easy to become dispirited and negative if things are viewed as one awesome hurdle. Imposing order on one's life by setting out a programme and creating a routine helps to bring back meaning, and will greatly assist the task of preparing the ground for the new life that has to be forged.

Those who are major breadwinners may feel, at first, that returning to work is a pointless activity, only undertaken because of the financial necessity. They may feel detached from their colleagues who, not having experienced the upheaval of a personal loss, may seem frivolous, their everyday concerns and problems merely trivial. Such feelings about others are understandable, but are not reasons for rejecting everyday situations. These are as much a real part of living as the tragedy that has been suffered. Besides, the responsibilities of employment can be immensely therapeutic, even allowing for an inevitably reduced level of ability and concentration for the duration of the period of healing.

For those who are not working, a small job outside the home can be an extremely valuable means of keeping in touch with other people, and will help to provide continuity and stability during the time of healing. This may be paid or voluntary employment. In fact, voluntary employment is likely to offer a far greater degree of flexibility, and where this involves frequent contact with the public, and especially help with the problems of others, this can make a considerable contribution towards achieving a readjustment. Knowing that one has helped someone, even in a minor way, can be a great boost to one's spirits.

The point of such activities is to demonstrate to onself that achievement is still possible, that one can make it by onself; albeit very painfully at first. Feeling that a job has been well done and that others have benefited as a result can have an amazingly uplifting effect.

There is a danger, however, that the bereaved may fall victim to activities which are completely out of character and which are undertaken in a desperate attempt to regain that which has been lost. Ironically, this usually only serves to compound grief rather than dilute it. Heavy smoking, drinking or casual affairs, for example, can be very much regretted later, although such regrets are, at least, an indication that the bereaved has realized there are no short cuts on the path of grief.

## FRIENDS

Attitudes towards the company of others will vary. Making new friends may seem difficult, even inappropriate, to some, especially during the early stages of a loss. It may be felt that there is an element of desertion, even perhaps of betrayal, of a lost loved one if new friendships are forged too soon. It *will* be realized in time that it is not possible to seek the approval of the lost loved one; that, in any event, the very idea of such approval is illogical; and that these ambivalent feelings must be overcome if life is to continue properly and not become a penance.

Those who need to seek out new friendships as a part of their healing process may have to bear the disapproval of those closest to them. Feeling constrained by other people's ideas of what constitutes an acceptable period of mourning can only set back the healing process of those who need this way of preparing for the future; it is *their* way of avoiding their lives becoming fossilized at the point of their bereavement.

When it is freely considered appropriate to seek out new friendships the next hurdle is often finding a way to meet people. This can be very difficult, especially for those who are shy. For a recently bereaved person, time and patience are absolutely essential. It can be helpful to seek the company of others in a situation which is not primarily organized for social purposes, for instance, evening classes, which have the additional benefit that the other members already share a mutual interest. Most importantly, it will allow sufficient time to get to know people without feeling any pressure to socialize outside the regular gathering. If it appears that there are no potential long-term friends, then, at least a new interest has been stimulated, and one will have gained in confidence.

Bereavement groups may be an additional or an alternative means of contact with others. During the initial period of grief, where finding the right kind of support is difficult and there is the feeling of having to cope alone, support groups can fulfil an important role. This is not to say that they can provide the answer forever or that they are the best solution for everyone. However, they are an important means by which healing can be assisted for many; isolation can be avoided and the deep hurt that is felt can be openly expressed. The first few meetings may not be easy; familiarizing oneself with strangers who share a common bond and eventually being encouraged to participate by sharing one's own feelings, can be exhausting. There may be a temptation, at first, to run away from such gatherings, but perseverence will pay dividends later. Realizing, too, that one will eventually be contributing as much as one takes out initially, provides an additionally positive element.

Bereavement group members often become a separate set of friends; even after members have long departed from the group, contact may be frequent. The only danger for some for whom making friends has never been particularly easy, is that the only friendships that now seem to be possible are those within a bereavement group. When social life revolves entirely around a bereavement group for too long a period, other group members should gently stress the importance of seeking new friendships outside the group. However, an organization such as CRUSE - BEREAVEMENT CARE (see page 207 for the address) will provide the right counselling and support for as long as is necessary.

## REAPPRAISING

Emerging from grief will often mean a reappraisal of one's values. There may never be a question of getting back to normal in the sense of reaffirming the value-judgements one had prior to bereavement: a part of life will have changed irrevocably. Perspectives may change; without the loved one the original purpose of certain goals may have gone.

'I was earning all this money for us both. I wanted to give her everything I could, because I loved her, and still love her, so much. It now seems a pointless exercise. I've thought it through very carefully and I've decided I have a lot to contribute by spending time with Voluntary Service Overseas. I've no family ties, and I feel that a knowledge of bricklaying will be of far more value in a Third World country than here. It's something I have to do.'

For most, of course, there will be neither the opportunity nor indeed the desire to make such a radical change of direction. However, there is likely to be at least a change in outlook. Old friendships and acquaintances, for instance, may no longer be sustained in the same way socially. The bereaved may neither be able nor want to fulfil friends' continued expectations of their contribution to the social scene. It is often the case that activities involving helping others become important and are undertaken with varying degrees of commitment. Often there is an increase in feelings of compassion and tolerance. Whereas, once upon a time, attempts by others to engage us in their problem-solving might have received a less than enthusiastic response, now they are given sympathetic consideration. It may be felt that, having made the journey ourselves we now have the experience to help another through that same journey, or indeed through any kind of problem. In *Recovery from Bereavement*, Dr Colin Murray Parkes says that the more people have lost, the more they will eventually have, to offer others.

Such reappraisal alone can never be sufficient compensation for the loss that has been suffered. Its importance, however, lies in the realization that out of grief will emerge the embryo of a new life. Such emergence will be gradual but each new step and each new accomplishment will bring with it a newly found purpose.

## RE-ESTABLISHING

Feeling reintegrated and re-established will not be a sudden transition. It will be a gradual, almost imperceptible process; however it is possible to determine whether the journey has begun and how far one has travelled.

One of the most positive indicators is the ability to think about, even discuss with others, those good times experienced with a lost loved one, without automatically feeling immense pain and longing for the restoration of the past. There may be tears, but as time progresses they will be less frequent, and the point will come where it is possible to indulge in affectionate laughter at and criticism of a loved one without feeling disloyal.

Being able to show genuine interest again in other people, their problems and achievements, is an important sign of progress. It may seem minor, but not having to check oneself continually from using the first person plural instead of the first person singular, is an important indication that readjustment is underway. So, too, is the use of the past tense instead of the present tense when referring to a lost loved one, whether in conversation or in private thoughts.

The ability to achieve things thought to be impossible without the help of the lost loved one is an immensely important indicator. It is confidence-boosting enough in the matter of ordinary day-to-day activities; where the bereaved person has been permanently confined to a wheelchair, it can be positively uplifting:

'I am finally managing to be my own person in a way that I never thought possible. It's not that I was made to feel helpless, it's just that neither of us knew what my limitations were, so we probably over-compensated. Recovering from Jamie's death has left me with the strength to succeed for myself, now. At first, I felt worse than helpless. That was because I didn't want to succeed. I wanted to be and to feel dependent. My grief, however, has also been my healing. I still am healing, of course, and I may go on healing for some time yet. But I am now realizing that I am developing into a more able person than I thought possible'.

'I have gained a considerable amount of self-respect. I have been dropped in at the deep end and am managing to keep my head above water. Because I have coped under these conditions, my self-esteem has gone up – my confidence has increased. I almost feel as though I would like to wear a badge on my chest proudly proclaiming "Look at me, I have considerable disability. I have suffered immense personal tragedy and, yet, here I am, still fighting, still going strong." For the first time in a long while I can say I am beginning to feel good and looking forward to the future.'

In the words of Kahlil Gibran (from *The Prophet*):

'The deeper that sorrow carves into your being, the more joy you will contain. When you are joyous, look deep into your heart and you will find it is only that which has given you sorrow that is giving you joy. When you are sorrowful look again into your heart, and you will see that in truth you are weeping for that which has been your delight.'

# 11 A Diary to Share

### by Doris Crowe (and Christopher Golding)

I

It is now sixteen weeks since that Saturday Tom died. I keep telling myself I should be getting over the bereavement by now – but it seems to get worse each week. This must be normal, I suppose, for other widows say it was just like that for them. Sundays are by far the worst days, particularly at tea-time. I don't know why I feel so depressed at this time – I leave some little chores such as watering plants or writing a letter for that period between half past three and six o'clock. It doesn't seem to help much, though. 'Only time,' people keep saying; I hope they're right, but sixteen weeks with a Sunday tea-time in each one – I've yet to see how the passing of time helps.

Most of the other days are bearable and they're sometimes quite happy days. Then all of a sudden little reminders are there which disturb the contentment; the sad moment I see his writing on a piece of paper inside his account book, or I pick up the waste-paper basket under his desk and it is empty. Little reminders which make me remember that it was only a short while ago that he left me.

The first few days and weeks were so busy with no time to ponder or dwell on what had happened. There were so many forms to fill in and letters to write and worries about how the financial side of my life would work out. Never in all our married life have I needed to worry about money. It was only since Tom's stroke that the responsibility fell on my shoulders. I had my own little financial world – the housekeeping money – and the baker and milkman, etc. were my only concern. Not for me the world of bank statements and interest and pensions and . . . Oh! the list seems endless. But, suddenly, I found myself having to write business letters and to

162

try and make sense of Income Tax forms! I know now I should have taken more interest in our affairs instead of feeling that because all was well in Tom's hands there was simply no need for me to worry about such things.

During the first month, the postman walked up our front path with his hands full of letters and cards. So many people wrote and I felt loved and cared for, thought and prayed for. Then it all stopped! A few of my dear old friends have stood by me and written again and again. They have telephoned and given me invitations. Cynthia, my neighbour, is always there if I need her. I don't encroach on her life any more than I can help, but she is a kind shoulder to lean on if I feel I'm reaching the end of my tether. I have replied to the mass of people who wrote, one by one, over the weeks. But now I don't hear any more. Perhaps they give me a thought now and then and they probably think I'm perfectly all right. 'She is free of the burden,' I can hear them saying, and, 'She writes in a cheerful style, so she must be all right.' It is true that I am free of the physical burden – these last four years have been tough – but, strangely, I don't think much about the difficult times, I think about the happy, healthy years.

I wish we had done some of the things we had planned to do but somehow never seemed to get round to doing. But I'm really glad we did some of the sillier things – such as giving Tom's mother our very last ten pounds in the bank after our return from honeymoon! Or going on holiday to Spain, every year, when our savings in the bank were under £300! Then the risk we took in moving house when his health was already showing signs of failing. I'm glad we came – he had one happy year, doing the garden and realizing the dream of many years. Oh, yes! I'm glad we did so many things together in our forty-six years of married life.

And now, I'm sixteen weeks into this new life called widowhood. I hope I can keep a cheerful outward me, until the inward me catches up and becomes cheerful again, too. This world is full of widows, so I'm not treading a new road, it's just that *I* have never been on this particular road before

163

and I'm finding it difficult to believe that it leads anywhere, but I'm sure it must do.


II

Two more weeks have passed since I last wrote, with two more Sundays, of course, in between. Thanks to our dear Vicar, they have managed to become better days. He seems to understand how I feel and knows when to ask me to accompany him to a place he knows I will enjoy visiting.

Last Sunday, it was to tea at the home of a lovely couple. They were so kind and matter-of-fact. I was welcomed as if I had known them all my life. It is funny how out of tragedy and heartache new friends can blossom from new directions. Bob and Ruth just seemed to understand my situation. It wasn't just because they must have been told who I was beforehand and what had happened so recently to me; there was more to it than that. They did not mind me talking about Tom at all and let me go on in my own way, without making me feel as if I was a nuisance. They seemed to interested and attentive and just listened to what I had to say. They asked questions about him in such an understanding way.

There have been some people who have seemed frightened to talk about Tom now that he is no longer here. It is as if he had never existed. That upsets me. Bob and Ruth, though, were so interested in Tom *as my husband*. The times we shared; the things we did together. That was really important to me. We managed to exchange stories about newly married life. It was so wonderful to be able to share laughter again. I enjoyed my visit immensely and felt so uplifted when I returned home.

This Sunday, our dear Rector took me to a church I had never been to before where a lay-preacher was giving the sermon. It was not so much the service or the sermon that I liked; it was just that I was with other people again. I suppose I could have been at any gathering, really; it wasn't so much the religious side of the meeting that I found uplifting, that seemed almost secondary. It was the mere fact that I could see others doing what they often do at this particular time of the week, and realizing that lots of people have to carry on with their lives, too. I wonder what they have gone through at different times? Perhaps some of them are going through the same as I am, now.

After the service, the Rector told me he had to go to a meeting nearby. It would last for about an hour, he said, and he would arrange for me to be taken home by someone else. I told him, though, I would wait until he had finished. The evening was so lovely, it was a wonderful opportunity for me to take a walk in the grounds of the church and to reflect on the day's events.

It cannot be said that this Sunday has been a major turning point in my life; but it has not been an insignificant day either. I think I have seen, perhaps for the first time in my life, that other people are more than just 'other people'. When I am out and see many people whom I do not know – as I and most others do everyday – people have, until now, always seemed just part of the scenery to me. I do not think I have ever given them that much thought before. But people seem so different now. They are so real and so alive. They have families, friends, lovers, admirers. They are precious to someone. We get exasperated with complete strangers for jumping our place in a queue accidentally; for bumping into our trolley in the supermarket and not saying 'sorry'; for annoying us with the way they speak, look or dress. How easily we can let such insignificances rule our lives and let the way we think of people be dictated by such silly things. If something were to happen to any one of them, there is someone else, somewhere, who will have to pick up the pieces, just like me. How my heart goes out to them.

So, two consecutive Sundays when I simply didn't have the time to feel so sad and depressed as I usually do. I'm sure the time will come when I shall not feel sad any more and the memories will have lost their pain.

III

Since I last wrote I have been busy. It has been a summer with a mixture of weather but I have been keen to get the garden into shape. You know, it was very much Tom's garden, I was just happy to be his assistant. It's funny, he always said it was *my* garden and that every effort he put into it was only for me to enjoy. He always said that if it was not for me being able to share the garden with him then there would be no point in him putting so much effort into it. I was queen of the kitchen and the household; he was king of the garden.

I became Tom's gardening student when he felt it was impossible to go on with his hard work. He had changed from being an active amateur horticulturist to someone who was just content to watch me taking over his old jobs. As I went into the garden today, and saw all the fruit ripening, I could almost see Tom sitting on his garden seat. He spent so many hours there. Many of those hours were lonely ones for him when I was so busy in the house. He did not seem to mind, though. His condition had deteriorated to an extent where he found it easier not to talk very much.

When I was gardening, nearby, he would say to me, slowly: 'You will not have to do all this hard work, next year. I'll be able to do the garden again.'

Most times, though, I didn't answer because I knew he would never again be able to do the thing he loved most. I think in his heart he knew it, too; but being the protective husband that he always was, he still wanted to shield me from what he must have realized was the inevitable. That is something which I hold very dearly. Even his terminal illness and its debilitating consequences could not stop him from acting as my protector.

I often wish I had boosted his fighting spirit instead of just remaining silent. He lived with faith and hope but I do so feel that I failed to help him sometimes in boosting his dearly-held belief. I suppose it is easy to say now but why couldn't I have tried to see things from his point of view? But, oh, even if we accept death as inevitable, when it's so close to us surely it is natural to want to push it into the distant future? How would I feel if I knew there was a strong possibility of my dying by the end of this summer? Surely, I would regard it as unreal and believe that whatever was causing my present suffering would pass and that I would live to see next summer, as well? But I still feel that if I hadn't just sat back passively and accepted the verdict of the medical profession I could have taken a more positive role in helping Tom. If I had felt there was just a tiny chance of his recovering I could have done more. There, I am making excuses for myself. It should have been up to me and no one else to boost his fighting spirit.

I have no regrets about the care I gave him. I *am* bothered though about whether I did enough to get him the best medical care. It seems so silly to feel the way I do, but I am constantly plagued by the thought that there may have been a treatment somewhere in the world that might have restored him to full health or, at least, have saved his life. I think of all sorts of things. Should I have gone to a faith healer? Should I have done this, should I have done that, should I . . . should I? None of what I am thinking seems to make much sense but I am bothered by this persistent guilt.

I do get some consolation, though, from the thought that many people have regrets and feelings of guilt such as I am experiencing, after losing someone loved so dearly. The feeling that more could have been done, though, seems to be an ever present burden.

## IV

Thursday was Tom's birthday. I caught the bus and got off at the stop just before the one near the cemetery. It's nice to be able to do that as it gives me the chance to prepare myself before walking in through those large Victorian gates. Everything is so busy outside and so concerned with carrying on life for today. Then, I go through those amazing gates and it's like being transformed into another world, the world of yesterday; the world of the remembered and the forgotten; those who have their graves tended and those who do not. As I pass each one it feels like being in a home for waifs and strays. You want to embrace them all by making sure every one of them has flowers and a cared-for appearance, but you know it's just not possible.

Then, I reach Tom's little plot. I get so excited just before getting there, as if I'm about to be greeted by him and we can then start talking about our good times together. But, of course, such a thing just can't happen. All that's to be placed there is his memorial and a declaration to the world that this is his final resting place. Up until this Thursday, it has always felt that part of him really was there. I don't mean in the sense of his physical remains, I mean in the spiritual sense. Part of him, spiritually, was still there. But, on Thursday, it just didn't feel like that any more. It felt as if he had really left for good, that his soul had really gone on to a better 'life. All that was left were his earthly remains, the unseen reminder of who he was. His disabled body had shackled him for four long years; but, eventually, he was able to unburden himself from it and has now left it there and is as free as a bird, free to meet his Maker.

I'm glad I believe in God. I just can't imagine how desolate I would feel if I had no faith in God. I'm lucky, I suppose. I know my faith helps me to cope with the melancholy feelings I may get. I have never asked the question 'Why me?', when life has brought sorrow to my doorstep. Somehow, I have always known that my faith would help me through the pain and the anguish and that there must be a purpose to suffering. I hope I'm not sounding complacent or that I've somehow been chosen for special favour; it's just that with my belief I find I am able to accept, eventually, so easing my path of turmoil and grief.

That's not to say that I do not question what is happening to me. There are many questions to which there are just no answers. When I question the clergy about the purpose of bereavement and suffering it seems obvious to me that in their hearts they don't know either. Replies such as 'God has His seasons', or something similar, don't really seem to convey an awful lot. It all comes down to making the best of what we believe in our deepest selves in the end.

I don't know what lies in front of me, any more than anyone else does. I only know that the situation I am in now is a part of my life and life is an ever-moving scene.

## V

It is three weeks since I last wrote and today is Sunday. I think Sundays are gradually becoming happier days for me, although I may be saying this just a little too soon; for the last two Sundays have mostly been spent away from the house.

Last Sunday, I helped to provide the lunch for a cricket team from London. They came to play the nearby village team that afternoon. The fact that they lost by a few wickets didn't seem to diminish their appetite, though. I have never seen sandwiches disappear so quickly! In the evening, I was invited to play the organ in the village church. So it was a full day for me and my thoughts were occupied with all the tasks that I had to undertake. There was very little time to be at home and to dwell.

This Sunday has been different, though. Apart from going to church for the early morning Communion service, I have been home all day. So today has been a very testing time. I have been trying to guide my thoughts into a different way of thinking. I have been trying to stop dwelling so much on the happier times of years ago and wishing that they could have carried on and to remember, instead, reality and how the *quality* of Tom's life had deteriorated. If he had recovered from his last stroke, then surely he would now be having to endure much more suffering and pain than he had ever had to suffer before. Could I really have wished that on him? Of course, if it had been possible to restore him to full health again, then I would have wanted to see him carry on. But the reality of the situation was plain. He was a very sick man who would never again be able to lead the sort of life he would have wished. Therefore, any thoughts I may have had and may still have about wishing he had survived, can only mean that I am thinking about my own loneliness and unhappiness and not about the reduction in the quality of Tom's life, had he lived.

However, if I realize I must accept what has happened to Tom, and that it has put an end to his suffering, then I must also learn to accept the pain of living through bereavement. I must have the courage to believe that the time will come when I shall feel a complete person again and my memories will not be blurred with inward tears and longings.

I must also guard against always seeing the past through rose-tinted spectacles. It would be silly to say that we had a perfect life together. We didn't always. We had upsets and sharp words; we showed irritability towards each other; we got annoyed with each other, in fact we experienced most of the things that surface in most marriages, I suspect. There were times when we were utterly fed up with each other and would have been glad to have run away from our life together. Of course, we never did, not even for a short while. The tie between us was so strong and so we were able to weather all of our private ups and downs just as we weathered all the ups and downs and the fortunes and misfortunes of life, in general. He was not the perfect husband any more than I was the perfect wife; but when I think about it, I reckon we had a pretty good partnership. And the ending of such a lovely partnership is bound to bring with it a great sadness, and I do feel great sadness, at times.

Last Saturday, the family came for the day. It was so nice to see them all again. There was laughter and tears, happy memories, sad memories and funny stories about what it was like to be growing up and what it was like to be a parent with a family that was growing up, with all the tears and tantrums, cuts and bruises, cuddles and hugs and kisses. It was the sort of conversation that only a close family would understand. It really was a very happy day. We all missed Tom, though. We all realized that he has played a major part in shaping our lives. We owe him more than can be said in words.

I do feel for my grandson, Peter; it must be difficult for him, when he is only nine years old, to understand what a death in the family really is. The memories he will have of his grandad will be only those of him as an invalid. I hope I shall live to see my grandson grow to manhood. I know that

Tom would be saying the same things as I am now, if things had been different.

The stonemason called at my request this week. It seemed strange, choosing a headstone for Tom's grave and deciding what words should be inscribed. I never knew there were so many types of inscription or so many different finishes. I've only ever taken notice of the words before, never how they've been put together.

Whilst I was doing all this choosing, I suddenly had a very peculiar sensation. The thought flashed through my mind, 'Why am I doing all this? Tom isn't dead!' They have recurred from time to time, these sudden flashes of disbelief and which I *know* are completely divorced from reality. Here I am after five months of widowhood, still experiencing complete disbelief from time to time! I wonder how long it will be before this stops happening. Perhaps it's a kind of brake. Perhaps I am expecting my recovery to be a little too swift.

## VI

Almost another month has gone by and it is nearly six months since Tom died. I have noticed a change within myself since last writing. It is difficult to define, though. I can only think of describing it as resembling a mist that is gradually clearing, giving me the opportunity to start seeing the hidden landscape once again. Instead of being made to remain immobile because of the almost zero visibility, I feel I am able to start making plans and to accept invitations. There is a feeling of being far more interested in the things I am doing, instead of just going through the motions of doing things because it is necessary.

It's early days yet, though, and there are periods when gloom will close in on me and my old enemies of disbelief and sadness return. That's when I find myself having to fight feelings such as 'He *must* come back because there are things I need to tell him so *desperately*!' I never really know what they are, though, until I start working out what it is I want to say to him. I then realize they are only silly little things such as 'Who do you think was on television, last night?' or 'One of

171

Andy's cows had a calf, this morning!' I can only suppose that it is his company I miss, for they are never anything of real importance. But these desperate moments *are* becoming fewer and further between now, and I feel confident that I'm going to be able to face the future, given just a little more time.

I must say, I am looking forward to my holiday in Sidmouth, next month, as well as a few days with friends at Bedhampton during October.

The Rector has taken me on several delightful journeys during the course of his ministry. I have enjoyed especially the services he has taken me to at Salisbury Cathedral. We are a small congregation at Sedgehill Church and so it is good to go to the cathedral sometimes. It is awe-inspiring, though. No wonder the cathedral-building Christians put so much time and energy into creating these structures. They convey so much of what belief really means. It also reminds me that the whole Church is a very big family and I feel a part of that family, I'm so glad to say.

Although, I have always written this diary in the first person singular I have never felt it to be right, somehow. It has been an effort. Now, I can really begin to write and think as 'I', instead of wanting to say and write 'We'. I make *one* cup of coffee instead of automatically making two cups. I set the table for *one* person, without the vacant place bringing me close to tears. I feel that my recovery has begun. I feel better both physically and mentally and I am confident enough to be able to think that the worst is over. This is something which I am truly grateful for. It has been unavoidable and I know that I would not have wished it to be any other way, but I just wouldn't want to relive these last six months. Those who are going through the same as I am now have my heart going out to them in a way that I could never express with sufficient words.

Perhaps I have realized that the way to full recovery is in not to hope for today when grief will be no more, but just to let life's compensations pour into the wounds like a healing balm. Then it may be possible to walk on the new road that will have to be trodden and to look ahead to the new life and the new opportunities that will arise.

I think I have now stepped on to that road. Now all I have to do is to put one foot in front of the other – and *walk*!

## VII

It is only a week since I last wrote in this diary, but today is a kind of milestone and so I feel it ought to be recorded. It is *exactly* six months to the day, even to the hour, since Tom died. I now become a war widow, officially. My War Widow's Pension begins and the temporary allowance I received for the first six months now comes to an end. The interim period is over and I am now fully launched into widowhood. My new life has begun and I *must* start walking along the road I have spoken about so much. I cannot stay at the stage of what is described by the world as 'newly bereaved' any longer.

Sometimes, though, I feel that all my efforts are in vain, for just as I am beginning to be happy once again and that life is still good after all, some little thing will plunge me back into deep despair; but I have to keep *trying*.

These writings of mine do seem to be contradictory. Firstly, I seem to be saying that I'm getting over my bereavement and then I say that it feels as if I'm not progressing very much at all. My mind is continually see-sawing according to how I am feeling at the time. It's so puzzling. It's so – oh, what's the word – *ambivalent*. Things *are* better than they were three or four months ago and I feel I am on that road, but I still keep looking behind me!

Yesterday, I received a phone-call from my daughter giving me my grandson's examination results. They were excellent. I was so pleased for him and his parents – and for myself, too! How I wished there was some way I could have told Tom. Oh, how he would have shared our delight. Perhaps he does know; perhaps, in some way, those who have left us can look down and share the things we are so happy about. Throughout my life I have had the feeling that my mother has watched over me, ever since she died when I was fourteen. God bless her.

It is strange how we always wish our children and our grandchildren to make a greater success of life than we feel

173

we have made of it ourselves. We want them to achieve more in life and to receive more from life than we ever did. I suppose it's a way of reliving our own youth, with the plus of a better life. We feel that we could have made more of ourselves, so it's a sort of compensation to see it happening to the generations following us. As well as success in education, I like to see other endearing qualities in my grandchildren. I'm so happy to see that my love of cats is present in Peter, my youngest grandson, although I sometimes feel anxious that he will have to face the heartbreak that keeping and loving animals will inevitably bring. Nevertheless, we are lesser people if we don't have compassion; if we don't love; if we take without giving; if we treat any part of the world with disregard.

I seem to have wandered somewhat from the subject of my bereavement diary, although that is a good sign, perhaps. I cannot go on writing in it for ever and I hope that life will not allow me to. The memories will always remain, but memories are not living things, and there is still life to live!

## VIII

I have no desire to add further to this diary, save for this, my final entry. Almost two months have gone by since I last wrote and during this time my calendar has been full of engagements, commitments and short breaks away from home. Now, I'm preparing for another week away with old and dear friends.

I am firmly on that road, now. The traffic lights that have been changing red, to red and amber, to amber and green and back to amber again, are now showing *green, green, green ...*! This is the way I must go and I'm not going to stop!

I must be honest and say that the pain does return occasionally, but it is more bearable, now, and I am beginning to accept it, in a way almost to embrace it, as I realize it has become a small part of the life that is to be. There are tears in everyone's lives; there is joy in everyone's lives. I cannot claim that I am any different because of my loss.

But I feel that I am able to accommodate the pain that I may always have and I now know that it will not come between me and the new life I have waiting in front of me. A life which no longer resembles just a block of crude granite. I am now equipped with the tools to shape that great stone into something definable and meaningful and it's already looking good!

My diary has become a very trusted friend; its pages remind me of the person I was and the person I have become. A person whose life has not been ended by her tragedy, but whose life has taken on a new beginning. It has recorded what bereavement is like for me. What bereavement *is* like for me? No, no, this is no longer true. It tells me what bereavement *was* like for me. With God's help, I *can* say that!

# 12 The Formal Side of Death

## A DEATH AT HOME

When someone has died in England or Wales, the death must be registered personally within five days. This is usually done by the next of kin and the information is recorded by the registrar (of births, deaths and marriages) for the relevant district.

The documentation needed by the registrar is:

1  The medical certificate stating the cause of death – issued by the doctor and given to the next of kin.
2  If the coroner is involved:
   (a) The coroner's notification – confirming or giving details of the cause of death.
   OR
   (b) The coroner's certificate (after an inquest) – giving all the particulars needed for the death to be registered.

Whichever one of these two categories applies, the certificate will be sent directly to the registrar.

A further nine days will be allowed for registration provided the written particulars to be registered have been received by the registrar.

In England and Wales all deaths have to be registered in the registration sub-district in which the death occurred or where the deceased was found.

Only certain people are allowed to register a death, and a list of such persons can be found attached to the medical certificate of cause of death under the heading 'Notice to Informant'.

176

The medical certificate of cause of death may have been sent directly to the registrar by the doctor, in which case it must have been received by the registrar before registration can be undertaken.

The registrar will be sympathetic and understanding and will make the procedure as straightforward as possible. One will not be pressured into giving snap answers to questions. The deceased's medical card will also be needed, but if this is not readily to hand it can be forwarded later.

# A DEATH IN HOSPITAL

The next of kin are informed by the ward sister, or sometimes by the police if an accident is involved. If the deceased is not a patient in the hospital identification by the next of kin will be necessary. The possessions will be handed to the next of kin.

If the hospital wants to carry out a post-mortem examination permission from the next of kin is necessary.

Where the hospital has been able to make a diagnosis the medical certificate will be issued by the hospital. If the hospital has had no chance to diagnose the case the person's own GP will be asked to issue the certificate. If this is not possible then the death will be reported to the coroner. A death that occurred during an operation will also be reported to the coroner. The coroner is then responsible for the formalities.

Where a certificate can be issued by the hospital, the next of kin are from then on responsible for making the necessary arrangements for burial or cremation. Registering the death is then carried out in the district where the hospital is located, and is similar to registering a death at home.

# A STILLBIRTH

A child who is stillborn is one who has been born after the twenty-eighth week of pregnancy and where there was no breathing or signs of life.

The doctor present at the stillbirth or who examined the body will issue a Certificate of Stillbirth. If a midwife only was present then she can issue the certificate. If neither was present then either of the parents, or somebody who was in the house at the time, can make a declaration on Form 35, available from the registrar's office.

Registration must be carried out within forty-two days of the stillbirth. Those qualified to register are the mother; the father of a legitimate child (had it lived); the occupier of the premises where the stillbirth took place or a person present at the stillbirth or who found the stillborn child.

If there is any equivocation concerning the child being born alive or not, then the coroner must be informed. (See also in Chapter 7, 'A Lesser Bereavement?', page 100).

## FORMALITIES AFTER REGISTRATION

Once the formalities have been completed various certificates can be issued. These are (for England and Wales):

*Certificate of Registration and Notification of Death* (incorporating form BD8). This is needed for claiming widow's benefit from the Department of Social Security.

*Standard Death Certificate.* This enables probate to be obtained. It is also needed for claims such as life insurance, pension schemes and friendly societies.

*Special Death Certificate.* This is for claiming any life insurance on the lives of parents or grandparents.

*Certificate for Purposes of the Friendly Society Acts.* To pursue claims from a friendly society.

*Certificate for Certain Statutory Purposes.* Used for claims under the National Insurance and Social Security Acts. It can also be used if the Certificate of Registration has been lost. In some instances probate will not be required, such as for all National Savings Bank accounts, including Premium Bonds, and here this certificate will suffice.

Make sure all the certificates that will be needed are obtained when registering the death. To obtain additional copies later will cost much more. For a recent death, application to the issuing registrar is made. Where a death occurred more than a year previously, a standard death certificate may be obtained from The General Register Office, St. Catherine's House, 10 Kingsway, London WC2B 6JP.

Once the death has been registered by the registrar, the Registrar's Certificate for Burial (the Disposal Certificate) can be issued. This is the necessary authority needed for burial.

If the coroner has been involved and there has been an inquest, the Order for Burial will be issued by the coroner instead of the registrar's disposal certificate. Where the coroner has been informed but there has been no inquest, the registrar can issue the disposal certificate but only the coroner can issue a certificate for cremation.

The certificate of authorization must then be handed to the person or organization involved with the burial, such as the funeral directors. The necessary arrangements for the burial can now go ahead. (Cremations are discussed on page 184.)

## PROCEDURE IN SCOTLAND

There are certain differences in Scotland concerning the formalities following the death of someone.

### Issuing the Medical Certificate

As in England and Wales, the responsibility for issuing the certificate of the medical cause of death is with the doctor who was treating the deceased during his or her last illness. If this is not possible, any competent doctor will be allowed to issue the certificate. If a medical certificate of the cause of death cannot be issued for any reason, the registrar can still register the death but the matter must be reported to the Procurator-fiscal. The Procurator-fiscal is not the Scottish equivalent of the English coroner; no such equivalent office exists. However, it is his responsibility to look into unexpected or suspicious deaths.

## The Procurator-Fiscal

The Procurator-fiscal may, after a short enquiry, be quite satisfied with the cause of death and the matter will not be taken any further. If additional medical evidence is necessary, a further medical examination will be authorized. In the majority of cases this is external only and a certificate of the medical cause of death is then issued. Where a post-mortem is considered necessary this can only be authorized by the sheriff.

## The Public Inquiry

There are no inquests in Scotland. This function is carried out by a Public Inquiry. The sheriff decides whether there is to be a public inquiry after the Lord Advocate (to whom the Procurator-fiscal is directly responsible and who has reported the matter to the Crown Office) has referred the matter to him. The inquiry is heard in the local sheriff court. The Procurator-fiscal examines the witnesses but the sheriff decides on the cause of death.

Where a death has already been registered and it has been decided by the sheriff that there are to be changes in the reasons for the cause of death, the Procurator-fiscal notifies the Registrar General who will then let the local registrar know. If the death has not been registered then the Registrar General will instruct the local registrar accordingly.

## Registering a Death

A death must be registered within eight days. A list of those competent to act as informants for registering will be attached to the medical certificate of the cause of death.

A death may be registered in the registration office for the district in which the death occurred OR in the registration office for the district in which the deceased usually resided before his or her death, but only if in Scotland.

A registrar will ask for the medical certificate of the cause of death. However, unlike England, if no certificate has yet been issued, registration can still go ahead. In these circumstances, the registrar will ask for the details of a competent doctor who will be able to issue the medical certificate. The other details required by the registrar are similar to that in England, but with a few additional details.

## Stillbirths

Under Scottish law a stillbirth must be registered within twenty-one days. The doctor present at the stillbirth or who examined the body will issue a Certificate of Stillbirth. If a midwife only was present then she can issue the certificate. If neither was present then either of the parents, or somebody who was in the house at the time can make a declaration on Form 7, available from the registrar's office.

Where there is to be a cremation, the death must have been registered. Those qualified to register will be found at the beginning of this chapter (see 'A Stillbirth', Page 177). In these circumstances, the certificate of stillbirth must be furnished by the doctor who was in attendance at the confinement or the doctor who conducted the post-mortem.

Registration must be in the district where the stillbirth occurred or in the district (in Scotland) in which the mother of the stillborn child usually lived at the time of the stillbirth.

If there is any equivocation concerning the child being born alive or not then the Procurator-fiscal must be informed. His results will be reported to the Registrar General.

## Formalities after Registration

Once the death has been registered, the registrar will issue a Certificate of Registration of Death (Form 14). This is the rough equivalent of the English disposal certificate. This is then handed by the next of kin to the person or organization involved with the funeral or cremation.

The registrar will issue a Certificate of Registration of Death which will be needed for claiming social security benefits. Other certificates are also available and are similar to the ones issued by an English registrar. Unlike England, however, copies of certificates are always obtainable from the local registrar who registered the death. They can also be obtained from the General Register Office for Scotland, New Register House, Edinburgh EH1 3YT, after a period of approximately twelve to eighteen months following registration.

# CARRYING OUT SOMEONE'S LAST WISHES

## The Wish to be Buried

Although there is a right for anyone to be buried in the grave-yard or associated burial plot of his or her local parish church, this is often impractical if not impossible. Consequently, many such burial grounds administered by the Church have been closed for further burials, but the situation varies from parish to parish.

Theoretically, the qualification is one of residency – anyone with a permanent address in a parish is entitled to be buried there. The situation, however, will need to be clarified with the vicar of the parish in question.

Burial for most people will mean interment in a cemetery administered by the local authority, sometimes by a private concern. Some cemeteries are owned by a particular faith (not associated with a parish churchyard) and are therefore restricted to members of that denomination. All local authority cemeteries have a part which is consecrated by the Church of England and reserved for such members. Some will have ground consecrated by various other religious denominations, again reserved for such membership. Cemeteries each have a chapel which can be used for any type of religious service. There is no requirement for any religious formalities at all, however.

In many cemeteries there are certain categories of grave. There is the public grave, which must remain unmarked by any memorial; its future use as a grave is in the hands of the organization owning the land. There is a minimum time before it can be reused, the exception being where a member of the same family is to be interred. However, the ground can be reserved for a further period by the payment of a fee.

It is often possible to purchase the right of exclusive burial in a particular plot. This is known as a private grave. Depending on the policy of the owners of the land, there may be a long time limit (say seventy-five years) or there may be a right granted in perpetuity. Memorials and headstones are an extra cost, of course.

There is also a type of plot known as the 'lawn grave'. Exclusive burial is permitted but there are certain rules governing the erection of headstones. As the name implies, the main part of the grave is covered with grass to facilitate mowing. Some cemeteries are converting existing arrangements into lawn grave areas by modifying the layout of graves. Before this can happen, though, objections can be made by the next of kin. They are notified in writing and are allowed a certain length of time in which to register objections. Consequently, such conversions take many years.

Before a burial can proceed the necessary documentary formalities must, of course, be observed. The necessary documents are:

1  *The Registrar's Certificate for Burial* (or the disposal certificate). This will usually be handed by the next of kin to the funeral directors and handled by them as part of their service.

2  Where an inquest has taken place *The Coroner's Order for Burial* will be received from the coroner's office via the registrar and this will then be handed to the funeral directors.

3  *The Application for Burial in a Cemetery*. This will usually be sent by the cemetery to the funeral directors. It is the formal application for burial and is usually signed by the executor or next of kin. It is then returned to the cemetery (again, all this will probably be handled by the funeral directors).

4  *Grave Deeds* in the case of a private grave. These may be held by the family concerned or may be held by the cemetery

183

authorities (or diocese). This establishes the right to be buried in a particular plot.

Details of the burial are entered into the burial register and a *Copy of an Entry in the Burial Register* is then sent to the next of kin or the executors.

## THE WISH TO BE CREMATED

A person cannot be cremated until registration has been completed or until the coroner's certificate for cremation has been received. At one time it was illegal to cremate a person if they had left instructions that they were to be buried. This is no longer the case. Now, even if detailed instructions for cremation are left there is no legal requirement for the next of kin to carry out such wishes.

Before cremation can be carried out there are four forms which have to be completed, although these are all on the same sheet of paper. They are Forms A, B, C and F and are issued by the crematorium authorities, but funeral directors usually have a supply. They are:

1  Form A – The Application for Cremation. This must be completed by the next of kin or executor and witnessed by a householder who knows the next of kin or executor personally.
2  Form B – this is completed by the medical doctor who was in attendance during the last illness of the deceased and who will have to see the deceased before being able to complete the form. The doctor is entitled to a fee.
3  Form C – The Confirmatory Medical Certificate. This is completed by a doctor registered as a medical practitioner in the United Kingdom for at least five years. The doctor cannot be a relative of the deceased nor a relative or partner of the doctor who has completed Form B. The doctor is entitled to a fee.

If the coroner has issued a Certificate for Cremation, Forms

B and C are not required. If the death has been reported to the coroner, it is essential that the coroner be aware that the deceased is to be cremated. Failure to do this may result in the incorrect certificate being issued (that is, one for a burial may be issued, instead). A reapplication will then have to be made to the coroner.

4  Form F – The Final Authority to Cremate. This is signed by the medical referee of the crematorium. Any fee is usually incorporated in the cremation fee.

Where a stillborn child is to be cremated, the doctor who was present at the stillbirth or who examined the body later will have to complete a special medical certificate. In these circumstances a second medical certificate is not required, although the crematorium's medical referee will need to complete the form of authority to cremate.

The crematorium will probably have their own form with regard to entering the arrangement details. Questions about the final destination of the ashes may also be asked for here. All the forms must be received by the medical referee at the crematorium by a certain time. The next of kin should make sure they know of the minimum time limit which is applicable to the relevant crematorium before a cremation can be allowed.

Similarly to the chapel in local authority cemeteries, there is a chapel which can be used by many different faiths. However, there is no requirement that a religious service be conducted, and if this is the case, then the chapel will be bypassed.

A Certified Copy of an Entry in the Crematorium Register can be obtained, for which a fee is payable. Guidance about keeping or scattering the ashes can be obtained from the crematorium.

## WHERE A PERSON IS TO BE BURIED OR CREMATED ABROAD

('Abroad' includes Scotland, Northern Ireland & the Channel Islands.)

185

If someone who has died in England or Wales is going to be buried or cremated elsewhere, the coroner responsible for the district where the body is lying must be informed. The registrar can supply the necessary form of notice to the coroner when the death is being registered and advise on where to send it. It is Form 104. If the registrar is aware before or at the time of registration that the deceased is to leave the country, the disposal certificate will not be issued. However, if one has already been issued then this must be forwarded with Form 104 to the coroner.

Once the coroner has received official notification, the body must not be removed out of the coroner's area for four days. If the coroner poses no objection, once the four days have lapsed the next of kin can carry out their wishes concerning the deceased. The coroner may even waive the four-day period if he so wishes or at the request of the next of kin or executors. The funeral directors will usually make all the necessary arrangements from then on.

Burial at sea is also classified as 'another country'. so the same procedure will apply. Permission must also be granted from the local district inspector of fisheries, who will advise fully on the matter. The address and telephone number will appear under the Ministry of Agriculture, Fisheries and Food.

For the removal of ashes out of the country or the scattering of ashes on English waters, no permission is required. Formalities at the other end, though, may be a different matter.

## BRINGING A DECEASED PERSON FROM ABROAD FOR BURIAL

When a British subject dies abroad either as an ex-patriate or as a visitor, the death will have to be registered in accordance with the laws of that country. However, the British Consul in that country can also register the death and this will lead to the advantage of certified copies of an entry of death being obtainable from the General Register Office. Failure to register with the British Consul will, of course, mean that there will be no official record of the death in England.

To repatriate a deceased person from abroad will necessitate contacting the Foreign Office consular department in London. Proof of death will also be required by British customs. However, the necessary arrangements will probably be undertaken by funeral directors who are experienced in this type of work.

The registrar for the district where the deceased is to be buried or cremated will require evidence that the death occurred abroad. This will be the British Consul's authentication of a foreign death certificate. If the death occurred in Scotland or Northern Ireland, the death certificate issued in either place will be required. The registrar in England will then issue a 'Certificate of No Liability to Register'. This will take the place of the 'disposal certificate'. There are three parts to this certificate.

Part A – is completed by the next of kin and declares the details of the death and makes application for Part B.
Part B – is completed by the registrar and states that the death does not have to be registered in England.
Part C – is completed by the burial or cremation authority and confirms that the burial or cremation has taken place. This is then returned to the registrar issuing Part B.

A burial must take place within a fortnight because of the requirement to return Part C by the burial authorities to the registrar within fourteen days. Where the deceased is to be cremated, the foreign doctor's statement of the medical cause of death should be in accompaniment. This, plus any other documents that were sent, must then be forwarded, along with Part A, to the Home Office, E Division, 50 Queen Anne's Gate, London SW1H 9AT. They will then issue a certificate to replace Forms B and C for the crematorium's medical referee.

# FORMALITIES AFTER THE FUNERAL

Property owned by the deceased person must not be disposed of before *Probate* has been granted (that is, proving a person's will). If a person dies without leaving a will, then the next of kin will have to obtain *Letters of Administration*. When probate has been granted, the persons dealing with the deceased's estate are known as *Executors*. When letters of administration have been granted, such people are called *Administrators*. In both cases, such persons are known as 'personal representatives'.

The personal representatives must let all relevant financial institutions know of the death, such as the bank (any savings will be temporarily frozen), the National Savings Bank (this will include Premium Bond holdings), and any building society involved. The local tax inspector will also have to be notified; so, too, will any private pension scheme. Briefly, after the grant of probate or letters of administration, the personal representatives will settle outstanding debts (funeral expenses are, of course, a debt), cash any life insurance policies and transfer or sell (depending on any existing will instructions) any property, shares, etc.

Any pension or benefit allowance books will have to be returned to the Department of Social Security (the address of the issuing office should be at the front of each book). It is a good idea to make a note of each number printed on the book, the exact name appearing on the front of the book, and the exact address. Any uncashed orders due up to the date of the death must not be cashed even if they were signed in advance by the deceased. Sums due to the estate must be claimed when the books are returned to the DSS. In the case of any war pension due, write to the Department of Social Security, War Pensions Issue Office, Norcross, Blackpool FY5 3TA; or you could contact your local War Pensioner's Welfare Office attached to the DSS. Quote the pension number. If no claim is made then no sums due will be received.

If the deceased was a former serving officer in one of the armed forces and was receiving a pension or allowance on the basis of war service, then any payment received after the death will have to be returned to the issuing office. Let them know the date of death and where the death occurred in order to claim the outstanding amount due up to that date.

It is important to contact the local inspector of taxes and ask if any tax refund is due. Quote the full name and if possible the national insurance number. A widow will also be entitled to a Widow's Bereavement Allowance. In the year of her husband's death she will receive this extra allowance to set against her taxable income from the time of the death until the end of the tax year. The allowance is also available for the following year, too, unless there was a remarriage during the tax year in which the death occurred.

There may be refunds due on unexpired portions of tickets such as rail season tickets or football season tickets. Contact the relevant organization for the procedure. Passports should be returned to the issuing office with a letter of explanation. Use registered post. They will return it, if requested, duly cancelled.

A vehicle registration document should be returned to the Driver and Vehicle Licensing Centre at Swansea SA99 1AR informing of the new owner. It may pass to someone named in the will or may be sold to a new owner, so in either case the DVLC will need to be informed. Don't forget to contact the deceased's car insurance company.

Action should be taken on any insurance policies. This will vary depending on the type of insurance involved.

All services received by the deceased person should be paid out of the estate up to the date of death. Telephone or write to each organization. If you phone, make sure you know to whom you are talking. The person responsible for the services from the date of death (telephone, gas, etc.) will then be recorded by each utility. Don't forget services such as meals on wheels or book clubs.

## BENEFITS AND ALLOWANCES FOR WIDOWS

The prospect of sorting out which allowances are available can seem bewildering, so it is essential to be armed with the latest editions of DSS leaflets 'Help When Someone Dies' (FB 29) and 'A Guide to Widow's Benefits' (NP 45).

## Help With Funeral Expenses

The Death Grant was abolished at the end of the 1986/87 tax year. There is now no across-the-board payment to take its place. However, in cases of hardship an application for a payment from the Social Fund (1) may be made towards funeral expenses. To qualify, the recipient must be getting Income Support, Family Credit or Housing Benefit at the time of the claim. A claim is valid from the date of the death, to up to three months after the funeral. If a claim is made later, but within twelve months of the funeral, payment will only be made if there is 'good cause'.

Certain deductions will be made from the payment. For instance, any savings above £500 (£1,000 if over sixty), will have a 'notional income' taken into consideration (1990/91 figures). This is worked out by the DSS. However, if funeral expenses are claimed within twelve months of the death of a husband, any of the Widow's Payment (see below) is ignored as capital. Assets which will come to a widow will be taken into consideration as will any insurance policies, etc. So too will any contributions from a charity or relative towards the funeral for *essential items*. Any non-essential donations, such as for a more elaborate funeral, should be ignored as capital.

## Income Support

If you have savings of £8,000 or less and are not in full-time work income support may be payable. Any claim will be based on your actual income (1990/91 figures).

It may be possible to keep some of the entitlements received by your husband. Advice on the exact position of a widow in these circumstances can be obtained from a Citizens' Advice Bureau.

## Widow's Payment

If your husband died on or after 11 April 1988, a lump-sum payment of £1,000 may be payable.

A widow must be under sixty when her husband dies; if over sixty, her husband must not have been getting a retirement pension. There must have been a legal marriage. If a divorce was in progress the decree absolute must not have been granted. The Widow's Payment depends, also, on a husband's National Insurance contribution record. There are two conditions, *either* of which must have been met:

1   Before 6 April 1975 the deceased must have paid twenty-five flat-rate contributions and these can consist of employee, self-employed, voluntary or a mixture of all three.
2   Since 6 April 1975, Class 1 or employee contributions have been based on earnings. In any one tax year contributions equal to twenty-five times the lower earnings limit for that tax year must have been paid. This condition could easily have been met in under twenty-five weeks. Class 2 or self-employed and Class 3 or voluntary contributions count as flat-rate.

The Department of Social Security will be able to supply this information. There is a time limit of twelve months to claim the widow's payment.

## Other Widow's Benefits

Full details of widow's benefits are in DSS leaflet NP 45. This will provide details of widows' pensions and the contribution conditions and the state earnings related pension addition. There may also be entitlement to a War Widow's Pension if a husband was in the armed forces and death was attributable to military service. Write to the DSS (War Pensions) at Norcross, Blackpool FY5 3TA.

When a widow has dependent children, Widowed Mother's Allowance will normally be paid. There is a husband's contribution record condition. This is payable from the pay day

on or after the date her husband died. There are additions
for qualifying children. The allowance is backdated for up
to twelve months; but additions for children can only be
backdated for six months. It is a taxable benefit.

When there are no dependent children and a widow is under
forty-five on the day her husband died, no allowance or pension
is payable. Only the Widow's Payment is payable.

When a widow is aged at least forty-five on the day her husband died or when her widowed mother's allowance finishes, it
is possible to qualify for a Reduced Rate Widow's Pension. The
full-rate pension is payable if a widow was fifty-five or older on
the day her husband died. The benefit ceases altogether upon
remarriage. It is a taxable benefit.

## Overlapping Benefits

**Invalidity Benefit** If a widow is receiving the Invalidity
Benefit from the Department of Social Security, then this
benefit and widow's benefits cannot be paid in full together.
However, it is still possible to continue receiving the Invalidity
Benefit providing this is made clear to the DSS in writing.

The advantage of electing to continue receiving Invalidity
Benefit is that it is tax-free, whereas widow's benefits are
taxable. If a greater sum than widow's benefit is being received
in the form of Invalidity Benefit, then by *not* informing the DSS
the same amount will be paid but it will be made up of the two
benefits together. Tax will be payable on the widow's benefit,
but not on the Invalidity Benefit.

If the widow's benefit is higher than the Invalidity Benefit,
the DSS will probably confirm by letter that Invalidity Benefit
is being paid as well. This letter should be kept safely for
any Inland Revenue query. It is also a good idea to carry
on receiving Invalidity Benefit from the point of view of any
Income Support and Housing Benefit entitlement; you will
probably qualify for the disability premium.

Claim this option when first claiming widow's benefits.
If you do not it is still possible to change to Invalidity
Benefit/widow's benefits by sending in a letter. It will start

from the payment date following receipt of the letter. The change cannot be backdated.

**Invalid Care Allowance**   ICA is presently taxable and the only advantage in continuing to claim it would be if a reduced rate widow's pension were the only widow's benefit entitlement. You would then be credited with Class 1 National Insurance contributions.

**Severe Disablement Allowance**   SDA cannot be paid as well as any widow's benefits. However, if SDA eligibility amounts to more than the widow's benefits it is worth claiming as, again, Class 1 contributions will be credited. It will also assist someone in obtaining the disability premium if they are an Income Support claimant or a claimant for Housing Benefit.

However, if SDA is not being claimed because Widow's Benefit will amount to more and Income Support/Housing Benefit is also being claimed, it is the *entitlement* to SDA which is the deciding factor in any disability premium decision by the Department of Social Security. However, regular submission of medical notes would be an essential requirement in such circumstances.

However, if one is entitled to claim SDA but is not doing so because of the overlapping benefit rules, and one is applying for the Income Support/Housing Benefit disability premium *for the first time*, an appeal to the Social Security Appeals Tribunal may be necessary. This is because the conditions stipulate that a person must be in receipt of a qualifying benefit. A claimant's case is likely to have to be proved.

A Citizens' Advice Bureau or welfare rights office will give guidance and will probably take up the case on someone's behalf.

**Special Cases**   The Social Security Pensions Act, 1975, and the Social Security (Benefit) (Married Women and Widows Special Provisions) Regulations, 1974, provide additional help to those whose marriages have ended by death or divorce. It also gives some help to widowers. The areas covered are

193

modified qualifying conditions for unemployment or sickness benefit and invalidity benefit.

The Department of Social Security will be able to advise if the contribution conditions for one of these benefits has been met. A Citizens' Advice Bureau or welfare rights office will also be able to assist if necessary.

## HANDLING SOMEONE'S ESTATE: AN OUTLINE

Although such a time dealing with the estate of a loved one may feel rather impersonal, it is essential for such affairs to be properly dealt with, both from the point of view of the remaining loved one's future security and from the point of view of satisfying the Inland Revenue, who, though sympathetic, have a duty to ensure that any taxes due are paid.

Many people will seek the help of a solicitor, even if the estate is extremely small and comparatively straightforward to administer. A solicitor may, of course, have been appointed as executor by the deceased. However, an outline of the procedure involved, it is hoped, will give some idea of what must be done.

Reference has already been made to executors and administrators (see page 188), the former being so named because the deceased left a will; the latter so called because the deceased left no will. Thus a person will die either *testate* (the former) or *intestate* (the latter). In either situation the persons handling the estate are called personal representatives. In both cases, the personal representatives have to obtain from the High Court a document showing that they have the legal authority to administer the estate. Executors will receive a document called a Grant of Probate; administrators will receive a document called a Grant of Letters of Administration (known for convenience as probate or letters of administration).

An exception to this rule is when the deceased's only property consisted of certain types of monetary holdings (see below), bank notes and coins, and personal effects (including a car). Anything additional to this such as a bank account and/or a house, must have a Grant from the High Court. So, in a situation not requiring a Grant – and this will probably be the exception – no solicitor need be involved. No formal steps have to be taken in proving the right of the next of kin to their inheritance. This will be the case even if a will has been left by the deceased. However, in cases of dispute, it is best to apply for probate and to settle the matter, thereby avoiding any equivocation.

The monetary holdings of the deceased which do not require a Grant are National Savings held with the Department for National Savings (up to a certain limit – check with the Department) and accounts held with savings banks, friendly societies and certain pension funds. There will be a limit on how much from each can be paid out to the person entitled before a Grant is needed, but the sum total can be much more than these individual figures. Checks will have to be made with the relevant institutions to see the exact rules of each. They will probably have application forms which will need to be completed and returned together with the 'Certificate for Certain Statutory Purposes' and the marriage certificate, if applicable. It is within the discretion of such institutions, however, to request a Grant before they will pay out any monies due.

Up until April 1981, it was possible to nominate certain types of monetary holdings in favour of another person, to take effect on death. This was usually possible for various National Savings accounts or government stocks. Any nominations made before this date will always be honoured on proof of nomination and production of a death certificate. There was no limit on the amount for nomination and so this procedure is distinct from the limits mentioned in the previous paragraph. If a large amount is involved proof of any Inheritance Tax liability may have to be furnished in the form of a certificate from the Inland Revenue.

The interesting part of these old nominations is that any subsequent will made by the deceased does not affect the nomination – unless a special form of revocation had been signed by the deceased. A nomination becomes revoked upon a subsequent marriage by the nominator, the death of the person who was the nominee, and the aforementioned form of revocation.

## A Brief Description of What Needs to Be Done

1 Ascertain exactly what the assets are and determine their value. (For obscure items such as furniture, the present market value, as seen, will have to be taken into account.)

2 The nature of any debts (the bill from the funeral directors is a debt on the estate, so too are the 'winding up' costs.)

3 Deduct the debts from the estate to arrive at a figure to be submitted to the Inland Revenue for the purposes of Inheritance Tax. The Inland Revenue, however, will have the first claim on any estate. They may require evidence of the debts that have been deducted.

4 Determine roughly the amount of Inheritance Tax (if any) that is likely to be payable. If necessary, arrange for a short-term bank loan. Duty will not be payable on any real property at this stage. The Inland Revenue permits duty to be paid in two instalments where real and personal property are concerned, ('real' being land, houses, etc.; 'personal' being bank accounts, etc. All real and personal property passing between spouses does not usually attract Inheritance Tax.)

5 Prepare the necessary documents required by the Inland Revenue and the Probate Registry.

6 Sign the Inheritance Tax documents and forward them to the Inland Revenue.

7 Settle the Inheritance Tax bill.

8 After having received probate or letters of administration send these or an acceptable copy to the relevant financial institutions in order to release the assets of the deceased. Any bank loan that has been taken out to pay the first instalment of the Inheritance Tax can now be repaid with interest to the bank making the loan.

9 Dispose of any property.

10   Settle any debts. (Any remaining Inheritance Tax on real property owing to the Inland Revenue is a debt to be settled. The Inland Revenue will advise how and when to pay.)
11   Make over any legacies in the will.
12   Settle any bequests.
13   Distribute the remainder of the estate in accordance with the provisions of the will or in accordance with the rules on intestacy.

Many people feel that they are quite competent to wind up an estate without the help of a solicitor; and where an estate is straightforward this is often possible. Not all wills are as straightforward as they might seem at first glance, however. For example, there may be ambiguities in the wording of a home-made will. There may be a business involved or the deceased may have been in receipt of income from a trust fund. There may be the setting up of a trust by the deceased for the remaining children. If the deceased died intestate and the estate is valued at more than a certain figure, the possibility of the remaining spouse only getting a *life interest* in the estate is a possibility. It is not advisable for a lay person to attempt to tackle such complexities.

Another rule upon intestacy is the sharing of an estate by *all* eligible blood relatives. This will be the case even if a long-lost brother or sister is living at the other side of the earth and there has been no contact with the deceased for many years. It cannot be stressed too strongly that financial embarrassment may be caused later on if the proper legal steps are not taken at the beginning of a winding-up.

However, if a solicitor is to be consulted, it is sensible to obtain an estimate of the likely fees. There is nothing mysterious about the legal profession, although this has been the impression fostered over many years by public and practitioners alike. A solicitor is there to provide a service like a builder, plumber or accountant. Few people would contract to have a new roof or repairs carried out to the guttering without first getting an estimate of the likely cost. A solicitor should be willing to furnish such an estimate, and if there is reluctance to do so then take your business elsewhere.

## A WORD OF CAUTION WHEN INHERITING PROPERTY

When one inherits a property it is obviously important to ensure that the name of the new owner is relayed to the company insuring the property. However, if the house is to be sold and is left unoccupied for more than thirty days, some insurance companies may impose a policy endorsement to the effect that cover against theft, vandalism, damage from burst pipes or oil leaking from heating installations, will no longer be given. If the house is to be used as a second home or is to be let to tenants, then different conditions will apply, of course.

Selling a house in England and Wales is not going to be possible within thirty days, so care must be taken with regard to such an endorsement on the insurance policy. Valuables should be removed from the house where possible. Applying to another insurance company may be difficult where an empty property is involved, so one may be stuck with this type of endorsement. Most companies will restrict policies after one month of non-occupation and all of the aforementioned endorsements may not apply, but do be warned.

# 13 Bereavement Compensation

This chapter examines, briefly, the kind of compensation that is currently available under the Criminal Justice Act, 1988. It also looks at the campaigns that have recently been undertaken to improve the financial position of those suffering bereavement as a result of criminal and other acts.

## THE PRESENT SITUATION ON COMPENSATION

The provision under the Act whereby the criminal injuries compensation scheme is to be placed on a statutory footing has been deferred because of a large backlog of cases. The existing ex-gratia scheme, however, has been the subject of revision from 1 February 1990.

It is possible to claim compensation from the Criminal Injuries Compensation Board if personal injury has been suffered as a direct result of a crime of violence in Great Britain, or on a British vessel, aircraft or hovercraft, or in a lighthouse off the United Kingdom coast, or within 500 metres of an installation in any part of the seas around the UK over which Great Britain exercises control. Compensation can also be claimed if someone is injured in the process of trying to stop someone from committing a crime, or trying to stop a suspected criminal, or helping the police to stop a suspected criminal. Case law has interpreted 'crime of violence' widely, enabling injury from a non-violent crime to be included in the scheme (e.g. injury or death sustained indirectly from a violent act).

If a loved one has died as a result of circumstances such

as these, claims can be made by a widow or widower, close relative, or dependant. Claims received on or after 1 February 1990 can also be made by a co-habitee, where the co-habitation has been of two or more years standing before the death. Claims can also be made if someone was injured in a crime of violence but died from some other cause. Compensation can also be claimed even if the attacker is immune from prosecution, e.g. for diplomatic reasons or insanity.

## Qualifying Criteria

The general conditions for eligibility are:
1   The injury must be serious enough to be within the minimum award amount (£750 in 1990).
2   The injury was not caused by a traffic accident where compensation is payable under an insurance policy or from the Motor Insurers' Bureau scheme (see below).

## Bereavement Award

There is a flat-rate bereavement award for the relatives of someone who has died as a result of violence (£3,500 in 1990). The only persons who can claim this award are the widow or widower, or the parents if the victim was unmarried and under eighteen years. These provisions cover deaths since 1983, even if the criminal injury took place before 1983.

## Traffic Accidents

If someone is the victim of an uninsured driver or a hit and run driver the Motor Insurers' Bureau runs a scheme for personal injuries. The MIB has agreements with the Government enabling such compensation to be made. Compensation is calculated in the same way as common law damages. If a driver cannot be traced, application must be made within three years of the accident. However, it is advisable to act as soon as possible. For details of the Uninsured Drivers' Agreement and the Untraced Drivers' Agreement contact:

The Motor Insurers' Bureau, New Garden House, 78 Hatton Garden, London EC1N 8JQ (Telephone: 071 242 0033).

## Violent Crimes Committed Before 1 January 1980

Injuries sustained more than three years before this time are not eligible for compensation. However, in exceptional circumstances this time limit can be extended by the Board. The CIC scheme was originally introduced in 1964, revised in 1969, in 1979 and again in 1990. Injuries sustained before 1 February 1990, will be considered under the terms of the particular scheme operating at the time of the injury, subject to any changes made by a later scheme.

## How to Claim

A claim form is obtained from the Criminal Injuries Compensation Board. Application should be made as soon as possible after the incident and it is not necessary to wait until the attacker is known or has been arrested. Where the alleged criminal is awaiting trial, the Board does not usually come to a decision during this time.

All applications must be made within three years of the injury or death, although late applications can be accepted in exceptional circumstances. The Board is sympathetic to late claims made in respect of children and mentally disabled people.

For the most serious cases legal help ought to be considered, the professional presentation of a claim, and advice on the level of award to be sought, obviously being of immense value. Legal aid is not available, however, but the Green Form scheme, allowing a certain amount of legal advice up to a limit, is available.

The CICB publishes a guide to the Criminal Injuries Compensation scheme called 'Victims of Crimes of Violence'. It is obtainable free from the Board at: Blythswood House, 200 West Regent Street, Glasgow G2 4SW; or at Whittington

House, 19 Alfred Place, London WC1E 7LG (Telephone 071 636 2812).

## THE FUTURE OF STATE BEREAVEMENT COMPENSATION

The Criminal Injuries Compensation Board, whilst it is a move in the right direction of compensating victims of crime, is really only the beginning and is ripe for improvement, especially with regard to the compensation levels awarded to relatives of deceased victims of criminal acts.

In May 1988, an organisation called the Citizen Action Compensation Committee (Citcom for short) began to press for solutions to the key problems in the compensation system of this country: the lack of access to justice and of specialized legal advice, the delays, and the often very low level of damages awarded. The President of Citcom is the Rt. Hon. Lord Scarman, the recently retired Lord of Appeal.

The Campaign promoted a Private Member's Bill which was published on 21 December 1988. It was presented by Lawrence Cunliffe, MP, and supported by other notable backbench MPs including Alf Morris and Jack Ashley, both Labour Members, and Jonathan Aitken and Dame Janet Fookes, both Conservative Members. The Bill sought 'to establish a [Compensation Advisory] Board to make recommendations for the levels of compensation awarded to injured persons; to place duty on the courts to have regard to such recommendations and to actuarial evidence in awarding compensation; *to increase the amount of damages paid in the event of bereavement* [my italics] and to extend the categories of persons entitled to receive such damages'.

In short, with regard to the section on bereavement, it sought to modify the rigid relationship qualifications for entitlement and to increase the financial awards to a minimum of £10,000 and a maximum of £50,000. There was also provision for linking the amounts to the Retail Prices Index.

Unfortunately, the Bill ran out of Parliamentary time

in 1989, and so none of the measures contained therein was placed on the statute book. However, the Government conceded during the passage of the Bill that the level of criminal bereavement damages should be reviewed, and they published a consultation paper during March 1990. At the time of writing, it contains three options: leaving the level at £3,500, increasing it to £5,000, or increasing it to £10,000. It is to be hoped that the still very modest figure of £10,000 will be the new level. The Bill's passage has at least met with a little success, although the categories of people entitled to receive compensation is not under review.

The address of the Citizen Action Compensation Committee is: 3 Endsleigh Street, London WC1 0DD (Telephone: 071 278 9686).

# Further Reading

## GENERAL

Collick, E., *Through Grief: The Bereavement Journey* (CRUSE, 1986).

Cook, B., *Loss and Bereavement* (Austin Cornish/Lisa Sainsbury Foundation, 1988).

Eldrid, J., *Caring for the Suicidal* (Constable, 1988).

Hill, S., *Family* (Michael Joseph, 1988).

Horn, S., *Coping with Bereavement: Coming to Terms with a Sense of Loss* (Thorsons, 1989).

Jones, M., *Secret Flowers: Mourning and the Adaption to Loss* (Women's Press 1989).

Kavanaugh, R., *Facing Death* (Penguin, 1974).

Kubler-Ross, E., *On Death and Dying* (Tavistock Publications, 1973).

Kubler-Ross, E., *Living with Death and Dying* (Souvenir Press, 1982).

Lake, T., *Living with Grief* (Sheldon Press, 1984).

Murray Parkes.,C and Weiss, R.E., *Recovery from Bereavement* Harper and Row, 1984).

Murray Parkes, C., *Bereavement: Studies of Grief in Adult Life* (Pelican Books 1986).

Owens, R.G., *Living While Dying: What to Do and What to Say When You, or Someone Close to You is Dying* (Thorsons, 1988).

Pincus, L., *Life and Death* (Sphere Books, 1978).

Raphael, B., *The Anatomy of Bereavement* (Hutchinson, 1985).

Staudacher, C., *Beyond Grief: A Guide for Recovering from the Death of a Loved One (Souvenir Press, 1988).*

Tatelbaum, J., *The Courage to Grieve* (Cedar Books, 1986).

Torrie, M., *Completing the Circle: New Ways of Life After Fifty* (Turnstone, 1982).

Whitaker, A., *All in the End is Harvest: An Anthology for Those Who Grieve* (CRUSE, 1986).
Winfield, P., *Can I Forget You?* (Constable, 1987).

# CONCERNING CHILDREN AND INFANTS

Burningham, J., *Grandpa* (Puffin, 1988).
Foster, S and Smith, P., *Brief Lives: Living with the Death of a Child* (Arlington Books, 1987).
Hollins, S. and Sireling, L., *When Dad Died* (Silent Books, 1989).
Hollins, S. and Sireling, L., *When Mum Died* (Silent Books, 1989).
Jolly, J., *Missed Beginnings: Death Before Life has been Established* (Lisa Sainsbury Foundation, 1987).
Jones, W., *Miscarriage: Overcoming the Physical and Emotional Trauma* (Thorsons, 1990).
Krementz. J., *How It Feels When A Parent Dies* (Gollancz, 1983).
Kubler-Ross, E., *On Children and Death* (Collier Macmillan, 1984).
Lonetto, R., *Children's Conceptions of Death* (Springer Publishing Co., 1980).
Luben, J., *Cot Death: Coping with Sudden Infant Death Syndrome* (Bedford Square Press, 1989).
Moulder, C., *Miscarriage – Women's Experiences and Needs* (Pandora Press, 1990).
Murphy, S., *Coping with a Cot Death* (Sheldon Press, 1990).
National Association of Health Authorities, *The Care of Dying Children and their Families* (NAHA, 1989).
Schiff, H.S., *The Bereaved Parent* (Souvenir Press, 1979).
Sternburg, F., *If I Die and When I Do: Exploring Death with Young People* (Prentice Hall, 1980).
Wells, R., *Helping Children Cope with Grief* (Sheldon Press, 1988).

# THE TERMINALLY ILL

Bright, R., *Grieving: A Handbook for Those Who Care* (MMB Music Inc., St Louis, USA, 1986).
Buckman, R., *I Don't Know What To Say: How to Help and Support Someone who is Dying* (Papermac, 1988).
Doyle, D., *Coping with a Dying Relative* (Macdonald, 1984).
Lamerton, R., *Care of the Dying* (Pelican).
Manning, M., *The Hospice Alternative* (Souvenir Press, 1984).
Saunders, Dame Cicely, *Care of the Dying* (Macmillan, 1959).
Wilkes, Professor E., (Editor), *A Source Book of Terminal Care* (University of Sheffield, 1987). (Available from: St Luke's Nursing Home, Little Common Lane, Sheffield, S11 9NE).
Winn, D., *The Hospice Way* (Macdonald Optima, 1987).

# CONCERNING WIDOWS AND WIDOWERS

Hemer, J. and Stanyer, A, *Survival Guide for Widows* (Age Concern, 1986).
Palmer, E., *Living and Working with Bereavement: A Guide for Widowed Men and Women* (Detselig Enterprises, Canada: Lavis Marketing, 1988).
Wylie, B.J., *Beginnings: A Book for Widows* (Unwin, 1986).

# Address List

## GENERAL BEREAVEMENT SUPPORT

Bereavement Trust,
Stanford Hall,
Loughborough,
Leicestershire LE12 5QR.
Tel: 0509 852333
A national network and
umbrella service for
bereavement support services.

CRUSE - BEREAVEMENT CARE,
Cruse House,
126 Sheen Road,
Richmond,
Surrey TW9 1UR.
Tel: 081 940 4818/9407
Offers a service of counselling,
advice and opportunities for
social contact to all bereaved
people and aims to relieve
suffering after bereavement and
to encourage rehabilitation.

Foundation for Black Bereaved
Families,
11 Kingston Square,
Salters Hill,
London SE19 1JE.
Tel: 081 761 7228
National Organization offering
advice and support to black
bereaved families. (May be
moving in 1991.)

Jewish Bereavement
Counselling Service,
1 Cyprus Gardens,
London N3 1SP.
Tel: 081 349 0839
Offers emotional help and
support to members of the
Jewish community. Provides
information concerning
Jewish bereavement customs
to voluntary and community
organizations.

Institute of Family Therapy,
43, New Cavendish Street,
London W1M 7RG.
Tel: 071 935 1651
Works with the entire family,
under the Elizabeth Raven
Memorial Fund, to offer free
counselling to bereaved families
or those with seriously ill
family members. Free service,
but donations are welcomed to
help other families.

The National Association of
Bereavement Services,
c/o London Voluntary Services
Council,
68, Charlton Street,
London NW1 1JR.
Tel: 071 388 2153

Aims to identify the many bereavement services operating in all parts of the UK, and to establish regional support groups for the providers of such services and to encourage the formation of such services where they are non-existent.

National Association of Victim
Support Schemes,
Cranmer House,
39 Brixton Road,
London SW9.
Tel: 071 735 9166
Practical help and advice given to victims following a crime. Also offers time to talk about the incident. Support for relatives of murder victims. Local support schemes throughout the country.

National Association of
Widows,
54/57 Allison Street,
Digbeth,
Birmingham,
West Midlands B5 5TH.
Tel: 021 643 8348
Offers comfort, support and help to all widows via its local branches throughout the UK. Widows advisory centres are being established to provide advice on welfare benefits, etc. Also publishes *A Handbook for Widows*.

St. Christopher's Hospice,
Lawrie Park Road,
London SE26 6DZ.
Tel: 081 778 9252
Besides being a hospice for terminally-ill patients, St Christopher's provides a bereavement service to families.

# BEREAVEMENT AND CHILDREN

Compassionate Friends,
6 Denmark Street,
Bristol,
Avon BS1 5DQ.
Tel: 0272 292778
Offers friendship and support to grieving parents who have lost a child at any age, including adult. Groups throughout the country.

Parents' Lifeline,
Station House,
73d, Stapleton Hall Road,
London N4 3QF.
Tel: 071 263 2265
Offers crisis support and counselling for parents of children who are critically ill in hospital. Also offers free counselling for parents and siblings who have recently experienced the sudden death of a child.

Parents of Murdered Children
Support Group (Compassionate
Friends),
46 Winters Way,
Waltham Abbey,
Essex EB9 3HP.

Provides emotional support and understanding to parents of murdered children via group meetings, visits, telephone calls and letters.

SOS Shadow of Suicide
(Compassionate Friends),
6 Denmark Street
Bristol,
Avon BS1 5DQ.
Tel: 0272 292778
A group within the Compassionate Friends, set up to help parents of children who have taken their own lives and to put them in touch with other parents.

Starlight Foundation,
10 Welbeck Street
Upper Thames Street
London W1M 7PB.
Tel: 071 224 0506
Aims to grant the wishes of children who are critically, chronically or terminally ill. Age range 2-18 years.

## BEREAVEMENT AND BABIES

Cot Death Society,
4 Mansell Drive,
Wash Common,
Newbury,
Berkshire RG14 6TE.
Tel: 0635 523756
Provides support for bereaved parents and supports research into cot deaths.

Foundation for the Study of Infant Deaths,
35 Belgrave Square,
London SW1X 8QB.
Tel: 071 235 0965/1721
(Helpline 0836 219010)
Offers personal support and information to parents who have lost a child through cot death. Sponsors research into the causes; publishes material on research findings and counselling needs. Encourages the formation of local groups.

Heart Line Association,
40, The Crescent,
Briket Wood,
St Albans,
Hertfordshire AL2 3NF.
Tel: 0923 670763
Support group for parents of children with heart disease. There is also a newly-formed bereavement support group.

Miscarriage Association,
PO Box 24,
Ossett,
West Yorkshire WF5 9XG.
Tel: 0924 830515
Offers support, advice and information to mothers who have suffered miscarriage. Publishes a newsletter and encourages the formation of local groups.

Multiple Births Foundation,
Institute of Obstetrics etc.
Trust,
Queen Charlotte's Hospital,
London W6 0XG.
Help for parents who have lost
a child from a multiple birth or
where there is a handicap.

Stillbirth and Neonatal Death
Society,
28 Portland Place,
London W1N 3DE.
Tel: 071 436 5881
Encourages research into
the causes of neonatal death;
has established a network of
bereaved parents willing to
help those newly bereaved;
stimulates awareness in
professionals and the public of
the needs of bereaved parents
and the long-term effects of
bereavement.

Twins and Multiple Births
Association,
41 Fortuna Way,
Aylesbury Park,
Grimsby,
South Humberside DN37 9SJ.
Bereavement support group
for parents who have lost one
or more babies of a multiple
birth.

# BEREAVEMENT SUPPORT GROUPS – BABIES AND CHILDREN

Association for Spina Bifida
and Hydrocephalus,
ASBAH,
22 Upper Woburn Place,
London WC1 0EP.
Tel: 071 388 1382

FORESIGHT,
The Old Vicarage,
Church Lane,Witley,
Godalming,
Surrey GU8 5PN.
Tel: 0428 794500
Pre-conceptual care association.

Listeria Society,
2 Wessex Close,
Faringdon,
Oxfordshire SN7 7YY

NIPPERS,
c/o Sam Seagal Perinatal Unit,
St Mary's Hospital,
Praed Street,
London W2.
Tel: 071 725 1487
Support group for parents of
premature babies.

Portsmouth Baby Lost Support
Group,
Rita Fraser,
Overall Co-ordinator,
14b Lovedean Lane,
Portsmouth,
Hampshire.
Tel: 0705 592958

Support, comfort and information for anyone who has lost a baby, as a result of miscarriage, ectopic pregnancy, stillbirth, neonatal death, or termination for foetal abnormality.

Support after Termination of Foetal Abnormality,
SATFA,
29-30 Soho Square
London W1.
Tel: 071 439 6124

Toxoplasmosis Trust,
The Garden Studio,
11-15 Betherton Street,
London WC2H 9BP.
Tel: 071 379 0344

**OTHER BEREAVEMENT ORGANISATIONS**

Campaign Against Drinking and Driving, (CADD),
'Meadside',
Shudy Camps,
Cambridge,
Cambridgeshire CB1 6RA.
Tel: 0799 84645
Support and help for families of people killed by those convicted of drunken driving.

Gay Bereavement Project,
Unitarian Rooms,
Hoop Lane,
London NW11 8BS.
Tel: 081 455 6844 (Helpline

081 455 8894, 7.00 p.m. to midnight)
Advice and support for homosexual people on the death of their partners.

**CARE ORGANIZATIONS**

Age Concern,
Astral House,
1268 London Road,
London SW16 4EJ.
Tel: 081 679 5110

Alzheimer's Disease Society,
158/160 Balham High Street,
London SW12 9BN.
Tel: 081 675 6557/8/9.

Asian People with Disabilities Alliance,
16 Saffron Close,
Hendon Park Row,
London NW11.
Tel: 081 458 1838

Association of Continence Advisers,
c/o Disabled Living Foundation,
380/384 Harrow Road,
London W9 2HU.
Tel: 071 289 6111

Association of Crossroads Care Attendant Schemes,
10 Regent Place,
Rugby,
Warwickshire CV21 2PN.
Tel: 0788 573653

BACUP: British Association of
Cancer United Patients,
121/123 Charterhouse Street,
London EC1M 6AA.
Tel: 071 608 1668

British Red Cross Society,
9 Grosvenor Crescent,
London SW1X 7EJ.
Tel: 071 235 5454

Cancerlink,
17 Britannia Street,
London WC1X 9NJ.
Tel: 071 833 2451

Cancer Relief Macmillan
Fund,
Anchor House,
15/19 Britten Street,
London SW3 3TZ.
Tel: 071 351 7811

Carers' National Association,
29 Chilworth Mews,
London W2 3RG.
Tel: 071 724 7776

Chest, Heart and Stroke
Association,
Tavistock House North,
Tavistock Square,
London WC1H 9JE.
Tel: 071 387 3012

Contact-a-Family,
16 Strutton Ground,
London SW1P 2HP.
Tel: 071 222 2695

Hospice Information Service,
51/59 Lawrie Park Road,
Sydenham,
London SE26 6DZ.
Tel: 081 778 9252

Independent Living Fund,
PO Box 183
Nottingham NG8 3RD.

Leonard Cheshire Foundation,
Leonard Cheshire House,
26/29 Maunsel Street,
London SW1P 2QN.
Tel: 071 828 1822

Leukaemia Care Society,
PO Box. 82,
Exeter,
Devon EX2 5DP.
Tel: 0392 218514

Marie Curie Cancer Care,
28 Belgrave Square,
London SW1X 8QG.
Tel: 071 235 3325

Multiple Sclerosis Society of
Great Britain and N. Ireland,
25 Effie Road
Fulham,
London SW6 1EE.
Tel: 071 736 6267/8

National Information Forum,
380/384 Harrow Road,
London W9 2HU.
Tel: 071 289 2791

National Providers' Trust,
28 Earl's Court Road,
Amesbury,
Salisbury,
Wiltshire SP4 7NB.
Tel: 0980 622944
(Via GP or similar only.)

RADAR, (Royal Association
for Disability and
Rehabilitation),
25, Mortimer Street,
London W1N 8AB.
Tel: 071 637 5400

Scottish Council on Disability,
Princes House,
5 Shandwick Place,
Edinburgh EH 2 4RG.
Tel: 031 229 8632

Sue Ryder Homes,
Cavendish,
Sudbury,
Suffolk CO10 8AY.Tel: 0787
280252

The Terrence Higgins Trust,
52/54 Grays Inn Road,
London WC1X 8JU.
Tel: 071 242 1010

Wales Council for the
Disabled,
'Llys Ifor',
Crescent Road,
Caerphilly,
Mid-Glamorgan CF8 1XL.
Tel: 0222 8887325

# HOLIDAY CARE ORGANIZATIONS FOR THE DISABLED AND TERMINALLY ILL

Across Trust,
Crown House,
London Road,
Morden,
Surrey SM4 5EW.
Tel: 081 540 3897

BREAK,
20 Hooks Hill Road,
Sheringham,
Norfolk NR26 8NL.
Tel: 0263 823170 / 823025

Disaway Trust,
6 Burlington Avenue,
Richmond,
Surrey TW9 4DQ.
Tel: 081 878 2054

Handicapped Children's
Pilgrimage Trust and Hosanna
House Trust,
100a High Street,
Banstead,
Surrey SM7 2RB.
Tel: 0737 353311

Holiday Care Service,
2 Old Bank Chambers, Station
Road,
Horley,
Surrey RH6 9HW.
Tel: 0293 774535

Jewish Blind and Physically
Handicapped Society,
118 Seymour Place,
London W1H 5DJ.
Tel: 071 262 2003/5

John Groom's Association for
the Disabled,
10 Gloucester Drive,
London N4 2LP.
Tel: 081 802 7272

Les Evans Holiday Fund
for Sick and Handicapped
Children,
65a Crouch Street,
Colchester,
Essex CO3 3EY.
Tel: 0206 561815

Margaret Hayles Foundation,
Plumpton,
East Sussex.
Tel: 0273 890243

(Raises funds to send
terminally-ill or sick children
on the 'Holiday of a
Lifetime').

Peter Le Marchant Trust,
Colston Bassett House,
Colston Bassett,
Nottingham NG 12 3FE.
Tel: 0949 81205

P.H.A.B.,
Tavistock House North,
Tavistock Square,
London WC1H 9HX.
Tel: 071 388 1963

Winged Fellowship Trust,
Angel House,
Pentonville Road,
London N1 9XD.
Tel: 071 833 2594

# Index

215